# Leading While Female

*We dedicate this book to our daughters,*

*Andrea Arriaga and Daniela Arriaga*

*Brittanie Stanley and Daina Stanley-Showers*

*Angela (Angee) Saucier*

*and our granddaughters,*

*Sofia Arriaga*

*Laila Crola Lynn Wilson*

*Holly Elizabeth Saucier*

*Charley Maryn Harp*

*Kiera Adoracion-Rai Jew*

*Jordyn Lindsey Jew*

*We hand you the baton. Continue the race and run like a champion!*

# Leading While Female

## A Culturally Proficient Response for Gender Equity

Trudy T. Arriaga

Stacie L. Stanley

Delores B. Lindsey

*Foreword by Thelma Meléndez de Santa Ana*

A Joint Publication

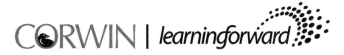

FOR INFORMATION:

Corwin
A SAGE Company
2455 Teller Road
Thousand Oaks, California 91320
(800) 233-9936
www.corwin.com

SAGE Publications Ltd.
1 Oliver's Yard
55 City Road
London, EC1Y 1SP
United Kingdom

SAGE Publications India Pvt. Ltd.
B 1/I 1 Mohan Cooperative Industrial Area
Mathura Road, New Delhi 110 044
India

SAGE Publications Asia-Pacific Pte. Ltd.
18 Cross Street #10-10/11/12
China Square Central
Singapore 048423

ISBN 978-1-5443-6074-4

Program Director and Publisher: Dan Alpert
Senior Content Development Editor: Lucas Schleicher
Associate Content Development Editor: Mia Rodriguez
Production Editor: Amy Schroller
Copy Editor: Amy Hanquist Harris
Typesetter: Hurix Digital
Proofreader: Sally Jaskold
Indexer: Sheila Hill
Cover Designer: Candice Harman
Marketing Manager: Maura Sullivan

This book is printed on acid-free paper.

SUSTAINABLE FORESTRY INITIATIVE
Certified Chain of Custody
Promoting Sustainable Forestry
www.sfiprogram.org
SFI-01268

21 22 23 24 10 9 8 7 6 5 4 3

# Contents

# Foreword

Reading *Leading While Female* reminded me of a time when I had just been hired to become the superintendent of Santa Ana Unified School District, after having served as US Assistant Secretary of Education for the Obama administration. As Assistant Secretary, I was blessed to have served all 56 million K–12 public school students across the nation. At that time, an article appeared in the *Orange County Register* in which I had shared with the reporter that I was the proud daughter of Mexican immigrants and that I started school as an English learner. I happened to look at the comment section of the online version and was surprised to read comments that raised questions about whether I had "papers" and if I was here in the United States legally, and ones that suggested my citizenship status be scrutinized.

The authors speak of the intersectionality of the different identifies we hold. Mine are female, Latina, first generation, baby boomer, and so forth. Yes, these identities impacted my work as a superintendent—and certainly in all roles as an educational leader—for the past 38 years. I've enjoyed the support of incredible female mentors and my husband, but I have also experienced the lack of support and disrespect from some leaders, unfortunately including some women of color in educational leadership.

In these difficult times, our multifaceted identities both serve us and make us vulnerable. At many levels of society today, we see individuals in leadership positions unfairly bash communities, misrepresent the truth, and reiterate a narrative that is demeaning to groups of people as it dismisses the positive constructive work that these communities have accomplished. The most important core values that have guided many of our actions as professional educators and as ethical individuals—truthfulness, integrity, respect, and collaboration—are too often openly dismissed. Sadly, we simply cannot depend on our national educational officials today to support our most vulnerable students. The meaningful work to which many of us have dedicated our careers is under attack. The consequent resurgence of outdated biases against women of color can only reduce the already slow growth of women into higher levels of educational leadership.

This is why *Leading While Female* is so important. In these difficult times, it is far more difficult, and for this very reason indispensable, to raise our voices, to stand up for our most vulnerable students, and to mentor and raise up talented women and women of color for positions of educational leadership. In this volume, the authors bring together words and ideas to better express a positive and powerful counternarrative to contest the systemic bias that now openly hinders women who seek high leadership positions.

The authors are all accomplished women and fierce advocates for students. They provide a conceptual framework "for ensuring equitable opportunities, access, and inclusion for all demographic groups into an educational environment." This powerful framework allows the reader to make sense of our very complex work in education. The Cultural Proficiency Framework is an important lens through which to view both our daily work and actions as educators and to evaluate the school district policies that guide our work. With it, we can better *assess* the responses to the standard queries: Are these policies supportive of ALL of our students? Do they ensure that women are provided with opportunities to enter the leadership pipeline? In addition, the framework provides the terms we need to better articulate the professional narrative to ensure greater access for women leaders.

*Leading While Female* is a positive narrative that can lead to change. The authors share the insightful stories of women leaders who participated in their research. I found myself nodding my head in agreement as I read their comments. Three elements arise from the research and professional narratives that will support the advancement and access of women to leadership positions: coaching, professional networks, and familial advocacy. This book is structured to provide opportunities for self-reflection for every educational professional, from the aspiring teacher to the sitting superintendent. It also provides essential, practical recommendations.

The authors offer educational professionals a book that will make a difference. As the baby boomer generation of educational leaders retires, they must pass the baton to a new generation of women who have different life and career experiences. *Leading While Female* will help transfer the leadership baton smoothly on a track that has become more uneven and where the rules of the game are changing. This book provides a clear call to action, for us to step up for our students and our peers, to articulate and defend the core values that we treasure, and to ensure access and success for the strong women who will lead this work.

Thelma Meléndez de Santa Ana, PhD
Former Assistant Secretary of Education, US Department of Education
Retired superintendent of three school districts

# About the Authors

Dr. Trudy T. Arriaga served the Ventura Unified School District (VUSD) for 14 years as the first female superintendent. She began her career as a bilingual paraeducator and enjoyed 40 years of service in education as a teacher, assistant principal, principal, director, superintendent, and university instructor at all levels. Trudy retired as superintendent in July 2015 and was honored by the naming of the VUSD District Office as The VUSD Trudy Tuttle Arriaga Education Service Center. She is currently on the Cal Lutheran University faculty as the Associate Dean of Equity and Outreach in the Educational Leadership Department in the Graduate School of Education. Trudy is the coauthor of *Opening Doors: An Implementation Template for Cultural Proficiency* (2015) with her esteemed colleague, Dr. Randall B. Lindsey. Trudy has focused her life work on the fundamental belief that the educational system has tremendous capability and responsibility to open doors for all students. Her leadership has focused on core values that ensure equity, access, and opportunity for every child and her or his family. It has been her privilege to assist school districts throughout the United States to align the actions of the organization with its stated values and principles in the effort to build a culturally proficient organization. Trudy and her husband, Raymundo, are enjoying this grand chapter of life as grandparents to Rayo Mana and Sofia Anuhea.

Dr. Stacie L. Stanley currently serves as the assistant superintendent in the Twin Cities Metro Area. Stacie has served in a variety of education roles, including classroom teacher, elementary school principal, math specialist, curriculum and staff development specialist, director of achievement equity, and director of curriculum, assessment, and instruction. Stacie is a Senior Training Associate for Cultural Proficiency and served as a contributing author for the text *Innovative Voices in Education: Engaging Diverse Communities* (2012). Stacie continues to seek and harness the voices that are missing from the table and to support schools and districts in doing the same. She earned her doctorate degree from Bethel University in Saint Paul, Minnesota, where she researched the impact of intercultural development on K–6 administrative leadership practice. Stacie is also a graduate school adjunct faculty member at Hamline and Bethel Universities in Minnesota. She lives with her husband and enjoys being an empty nester, taking long walks, and spending time with their grandchildren.

**Dr. Delores B. Lindsey** retired as Assistant Professor of Educational Administration at California State University, San Marcos; however, she has not retired from the educational profession. Using the lens of Cultural Proficiency, Dr. Lindsey helps educational leaders examine their policies and practices, as well as their individual beliefs and values about cross-cultural communication. Delores challenges educators to develop socially just practices and view diversity as an asset to be nurtured. She coaches educators to develop their own inquiry and action research. Her favorite reflective questions are *Who are we?* and *Are we who we say we are?* She serves schools, districts, and county offices as an Adaptive Schools Training Associate, a Cognitive Coach Training Associate, and a consultant to develop culturally proficient educators and schools. Recent publications she has been a part of include *A Culturally Proficient Response to the Common Core: Ensuring Equity Through Professional Learning* (2015), *Culturally Proficient Inclusive Schools: All Means ALL!* (2018), and the second edition of *Culturally Proficient Coaching* (2020).

# Introduction

## Identifying Pitfalls and Pipelines

*If there's a book that you want to read and it hasn't been written yet, then you must write it.*

—Toni Morrison

We honor the words of Toni Morrison as a woman who educated, inspired, and nurtured us through her written works. As three educational leaders, we wanted to read *this* book, so we wrote it. We present this book, which is written by women for women *and* men who support each other as educational leaders.

## PURPOSES OF THIS BOOK

Just to be clear, this is not a book about how to get a leadership job. This is not a book about fixing or transforming women into male managers or mindsets. The purposes of this book are as follows:

- To identify barriers that many women face as they strive for positions in educational leadership
- To clarify support factors that propelled some women "to the top"
- To offer educational leaders counternarratives to the status quo master narratives of male-dominated leadership roles
- To highlight the need and value for highly qualified women educational leaders

*Leading While Female* means working together with female and male colleagues who are also grounded in values for equity. We propose that by sharing these barriers, support factors, and intentional actions more women leaders today will interrupt current dominant narratives with their new stories of challenges and success. We intend for the book's title to be eye-catching, yet somber. We do understand the depth and weight of the impact of being profiled and stereotyped. We include counternarratives to help change the current and master narrative and lead the way for future generations of women leaders.

While this book intends to encourage each one of us to stay true to our authentic selves and to recognize that being a female is an asset in leadership, we are not suggesting that women transform, mold, or model the perceived notion of what a leader looks like. We emphasize the performance of the leader. She is, in fact, *Leading While Female*!

## FOR WHOM IS THIS BOOK WRITTEN?

The book is grounded in the research of feminism, intersectionality, educational leadership, and Cultural Proficiency. The Cultural Proficiency Framework is the lens of equity through which many male and female educational leaders examine their professional work and live their personal lives. The book is written for educational leaders who want to join us in *intentionally remaking a system that long ago put men in charge of women, not by happenstance, but by design* (Chiefs for Change, 2019, p. 3).

Audiences for this book include, but are not limited to, the following:

- Aspiring female educational leaders: Relevant and current stories of educational female leaders will assist in navigating the systems as you bring your unique and diverse goals, experience, preparation, and expertise to the front of the room.

- Male leaders: As you read the experiences of women, you will grow as culturally competent leaders and feminists. This is your opportunity to use your platforms to ensure opportunities for others. The entire book is relevant to your role as an ally, advocate, and mentor. Specifically, Chapter 6 is written to assist you with strategies, best practices, and intentional actions.

- Men, women, women of color, and educational leaders: Throughout the book, we offer strategies and action steps to establish gender equity and assist in the restructuring of cultural and systemic factors in all human aspects of the organization, with an emphasis on the female educational leader. Implementation of the strategies and action steps will assist in disrupting gender inequities within your organization.

- Women, including women of color, as emerging leaders: Given the lack of research for women of color, we purposefully share results of new studies that include stories of challenges and successes for recruitment and hiring practices inclusive of all women leaders.

## COMPELLING DATA REQUIRE COMPELLING QUESTIONS

The question we have for female and male educational leaders is this: *Are you a barrier (pitfall) or a support factor (pipeline) for women on their educational leadership career journeys?*

Our best reporting shows that women make up 75% of teachers, 52% of principals, and *fewer than* 25% of superintendents. We can safely say that women are doing the work of classroom teaching while, disproportionately, men are making administrative and leadership decisions (Fugler, 2015; NCES, 2018; Superville, 2016).

While the teaching population currently is nowhere near to representing the racial diversity of America's students, many female educators concur that increasing the number of African American and Latino teachers is a higher priority than simply bringing more men into the job of teaching. Of course, some women may not be so eager to open the educational leadership positions to more men. Christine L. Williams, a professor of sociology at the University of Texas, indicated that men teachers tend to be promoted more quickly into administrative positions than women. Williams (1992) studied and identified the so-called "glass escalator" (p. 256) as the advantages and pressures that men experience in a female-dominated field. She also noted another assumption that goes along with the glass escalator metaphor is that men are better suited as leaders than women. Her first coining of the phrase *glass escalator* implied a stable work environment and omitted the role that intersectionality (e.g., race, gender, class) plays for women. Williams argued that one way to get more men in the teaching profession was simply to improve work conditions and upgrade pay scales. However, in her current research, Williams

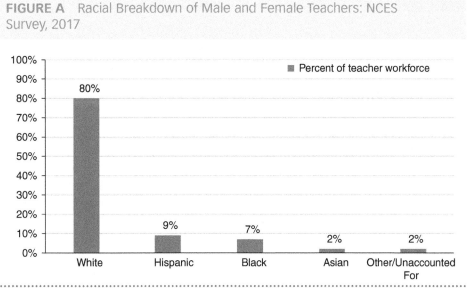

**FIGURE A**   Racial Breakdown of Male and Female Teachers: NCES Survey, 2017

SOURCE: NCES, 2018.

admits the problem of fewer women in leadership roles is much more complex than she originally studied. She now argues that new concepts and approaches are needed to study gender inequity in the 21st century workplace (Williams, 2013). We agree and contend that values and beliefs about why women leaders are needed in schools and districts outrank the argument for increasing numbers for the sake of statistics. We also contend that, taking all evidence into consideration, the lack of women in positional leadership roles is predominantly due to an inherent bias against women as leaders.

## PITFALLS ARE PERSISTENT

Since 2018, many women have called attention to workplace conditions of harassment and discrimination using the #MeToo movement. As we reflect on the movement, we ask this question: *Did we women actually help ourselves?* We learned that some men may take all of that energy and information in a different direction than women had hoped. This different direction might seriously impede women's progress in the workplace. How?

According to a 2019 study conducted by SurveyMonkey and LeanIn.org, more men have felt uncomfortable mentoring women at work because of #MeToo (Gebhardt, 2019). The survey, conducted in February and March of 2019, collected US data from 5,182 adults, ages 18 and older, employed full- or part-time. Of that sample, 2,421 were men. The results reported that 60% of male managers feel uncomfortable working alone with women, including mentorship, one-on-one meetings, and socializing, which is a 14% increase from 2018 US data. The 2019 report indicated that nearly half of all male managers said they would feel uncomfortable socializing with women outside of work, a 12% increase over 2018. Importantly, a combined 86% of men have avoided *one or more* of the following:

- Mentoring women
- Being mentored by women
- Going to evening work-related events with a woman from work
- Working alone with a woman
- Socializing or traveling alone with a woman from work

Obviously, these reactions by male mentors can have catastrophic impacts on a woman's career. Sheryl Sandberg, CEO of Facebook and LeaningIn .org, said of the survey results, *I really think we are facing a very serious crisis for women in getting promoted* (McGregor, 2019). Although the SurveyMonkey study (Gebhardt, 2019) and Sandberg's comments were applied to the broader sector of corporate employment, we believe that lessons from these sources can be applied to women in educational leadership roles.

What about careers of women in educational leadership? When do typical mentoring conversations occur? Generally speaking, mentees or mentors request one-on-one, closed-door conversations. Often, the conversations are away from campus at conferences or lunch/dinner conversations. Is the problem the time, place, and appearance for the conversations, or is it the behaviors of the mentors and mentees during the conversations? Let's assume the problem is that when men, by virtue of their privilege and entitlement in a sexist society, experience discomfort with vulnerability, they become reticent to engage in a confidential, closed-door conversation with women. The consequences of their unwillingness to change their behaviors are denunciations of opportunities for women. So, once again, women are being denied prospects and people for mentoring that may lead to possible promotions.

Women, especially women of color, in high-level, educational leadership positions are often viewed as exceptions rather than the rule. Female principals and superintendents are viewed as exceptional and extraordinary, whereas their male counterparts, especially White males, are seen as ordinary leaders who were in the right place at the right time. Male principals and superintendents are expected to be promoted because they've proven themselves to fit the mold of success. Their male mentors prepared them well to serve in the same system from which the mentor came. The pipelines for promotion are smooth. The expectations are clear, the rules are the same, and the work environment is familiar and comfortable. So how important and different are mentors for women and male leaders?

## PIPELINES FOR GENDER EQUITY: LESSONS FROM THE CORPORATE MODEL

The corporate world offers us a similar model for female and male educational leaders and their mentors. As in educational leadership, even though corporate women are mentored and sponsored, they're not being promoted at the same rate as men. As is widely reported, women make up 49.5% of the world's population and 50.5% of the US population. Increasingly, more women enter the workforce. However, from the initial stage of recruitment to the promotion stage, females encounter barriers throughout the workplace. Irrespective of increasing discussions about diversity and inclusion in organizations, women in leadership roles are still in the minority. Females continue to receive fewer opportunities than their male counterparts to spotlight their full potential. Researchers Shruti Sud and Apurv Amanesh (2019) indicated female corporate employees must work harder and prove themselves repeatedly as they work their way up to senior positions: *While 75% of businesses had at least one woman in a senior management role in 2018, compared to 66% in 2017, women still hold only 24% of senior roles* (para. 2).

The 2008 Corporate Catalyst (Ibarra, Carter, & Silva, 2010), a study of more than 4,000 high-potential corporate male and female leaders, revealed that more women than men had mentors—yet women were less likely to advance in their careers at the rate men advance, mainly because women and men were not actively mentored and sponsored in the same way. Although the study reported more women than men to have mentors, the women's mentors were positioned with less organizational clout. Not surprisingly, the study showed women to be at a disadvantage because the more senior the mentor, the faster the mentee's career advancement. Additionally, the 2010 follow-up survey revealed that the men had received 15% more promotions. These data indicated that even when women received support and guidance, mentoring relationships weren't leading to promotions for them in the same way they were for men.

Follow-up interviews with potential leaders showed that men and women alike received valuable career advice from their mentors; however, men were more likely to describe having sponsors in addition to their mentors. Many women explained how mentoring relationships helped them understand themselves, their preferred styles of operating, and ways they might need to change as they moved up the leadership ladder. However, men told stories about how their bosses and informal mentors helped them plan their moves and take charge in new roles, as well as endorsed their authority publicly. As one male mentee recounted, *My boss said, "You are ready for a general management job. You can do it. Now we need to find you a job. What are the tricks we need to figure out?"*

Mentoring and sponsoring are recognized as being integral to advancement into leadership roles. Ibarra et al. (2010) analyzed hundreds of studies and concluded that people derive more satisfaction from mentoring but certainly need sponsorship. Without sponsorship, a person is likely to be overlooked for promotion, regardless of his or her competence and performance—particularly at midcareer and beyond, when competition for promotions increases. The researchers of the potential leaders' study summarized the data with this key observation: The assertive, authoritative, dominant behaviors that people associate with leadership are frequently deemed less attractive in women.

Male mentors who have never faced this dilemma themselves may be hard-pressed to provide useful advice. As one of the study's interview participants described, even well-intended mentors have trouble helping women navigate the fine line between being *not aggressive enough* or *lacking in presence* and being *too aggressive* or *too controlling*. She explained the challenge of deal-ing with conflicting expectations from two different bosses:

> My old boss told me, "If you want to move up, you have to change your style. You are too brutal, too demanding, too tough, too clear, and not participative enough." My new boss is different: He drives performance, values speed. Now I am told, "You have to be more demanding." I was really working on being more indirect, but now I will try to combine the best of both.

> *My old boss told me, "If you want to move up, you have to change your style. You are too brutal, too demanding, too tough, too clear, and not participative enough."*

Ibarra and colleagues (2010) found that male sponsors can be taught to recognize such gender-related dilemmas. One of the large companies in the study has a reciprocal mentoring program. The program is described as a cross-gender mentoring initiative designed to support the company's overall diversity plan by connecting individuals to discover unique strengths of each gender. Women in that program have been promoted at higher rates than other high-potential women at the company, in part because the senior male mentors serve as career sponsors and have learned to manage their unconscious biases (Ibarra et al., 2010; Johnson & Smith, 2018).

The literature is clear that corporations value equity and diversity in the workplace; however, there has been little action to increase recruitment and promotions for women leaders (Sud & Amanesh, 2019). Mission statements and equitable and nondiscriminatory documents are drafted only for compliance requirements. Jennifer W. Martineau and Portia R. Mount (2019), who coauthored the book *Kick Some Glass: 10 Ways Women Succeed at Work on Their Own Terms*, write that HR directors could proactively recruit a pool of candidates that is at least 50% women before starting the selection process. They also stated that organizations should look at the glass ceiling as a systematic issue and not as an interpersonal or individual problem. They reiterate that leaders need to implement structured systems and practices to break glass ceilings and make space for women.

Until the glass ceiling is shattered, Martineau and Mount (2019) contend that women take charge of their own growth and success. The coauthors interviewed a broad array of successful male and female leaders. From their extensive research, the following themes/actions emerged for females:

- Understand your context.
- Uncover what you really want.
- Discover your definition of success.
- Identify your strengths and weaknesses.
- Set goals for yourself to overcome the glass ceiling barriers.

Martineau and Mount (2019) stated clearly that their recommended actions are not given to *fix women*, but rather to help motivate women leaders to overcome barriers and grow their career. Although we as coauthors feel the corporate model and accompanying data are important to know and study, we also want to caution our readers about the absence of data regarding LGBTQAI+ and career advancement. We also realize that much of the data from the studies we reviewed are self-reported data and that sexual orientation or identity are categories not included in questionnaires or interviews.

## Reflection

What might be some lessons educational leaders can learn from these corporate studies? In what ways do these recommended actions support your career planning for overcoming personal and institutional barriers? What's missing from these reports that's important for educational leaders to know?

_____

_____

_____

_____

_____

## Pipelines for Gender Equity: The Importance of Men Supporting Women

Educational mentors often are members of professional education organizations and volunteer to mentor emerging leaders. Typically, mentors are retired superintendents, other district office administrators, principals, or university professors of education leadership. Since the majority of these positions have been held by White males over the years, then logically, most leadership mentors are White men. As coauthors, we conducted interviews with women leaders and asked about their mentors, who were either assigned to them or volunteered to mentor them: *What were your experiences with your mentors? Were they support factors or barriers along your career path?* Some of their responses follow:

> *Most of my mentors have been males . . . and I had a male mentor who I deeply respected. At that time, I was a high school assistant principal looking to be a high school principal, and he told me . . . "Don't apply for that. Women are not high school principals. Apply for middle school principals." So after that, well, you know . . . I became a high school principal.*
>
> —African American female assistant superintendent

> *I've had many mentors in my life . . . all of my mentors have been men. And when I think of the barriers in my life in becoming a woman leader, with all due respect, many of the barriers I experienced were other women—women not welcoming me into the room, women not applauding me for my efforts. I was always kind of trying to fit in, get in, be invited in. And so, as we come together*

*as women . . . [we need] to recognize that how in the world are we going to move forward when we don't support each other?*

—White female superintendent

> **And when I think of the barriers in my life in becoming a woman leader, with all due respect, many of the barriers I experienced were other women—women not welcoming me into the room, women not applauding me for my efforts.**

*So I was engaging in a conversation to pair up a protégé with a mentor—a mentee with a mentor. And it was very interesting because there were males and females in both sides. But it was so telling: A female principal was matched with a person who was at the next level up, a Director mentor. And then a male principal immediately was matched to a Superintendent mentor because they see him as a superintendent in the future.*

—African American female assistant superintendent

> **A female principal was matched with a person who was at the next level up, a Director mentor. And then a male principal immediately was matched to a Superintendent mentor because they see him as a superintendent in the future.**

*One thing men do really, really well is networking. Men have friends that they've had for 25 years—they network; they know each other; they bring each other to each other's districts. And so, I noticed the male candidates going from dean to assistant superintendent (I'm in on the final interviews because there's nothing more important to me than our leadership team). And it kept being—the first few that we did were their friends. And I keep saying, How are there no women? Why are no women making it in? And so then I said, Well, let me screen those, so I sat through the next interviews, right? I had to say that—it's not a board policy, so I had to say— any leadership positions for our interviewees, I want 50–50 women and I want 50–50 diverse. That's it. Don't bring me any people to interview, any candidates, unless it's 50–50. And that changed the way we did business. I've hired eight women since then because when women are given the opportunity, they can do very, very well.*

—Latina superintendent

> ***I've hired eight women since then because when women are given the opportunity, they can do very, very well.***

*I think I've had so many more supports than . . . barriers. Well, my husband is the most supportive person in the whole wide world, and that's why I'm able to do what I can do.*

—White female principal

*All of the folks who've mentored me, male and female, have helped me be courageous. They've helped me make decisions that were outside of the box. And they've helped me with the strategies to do that right.*

—African American female director of instruction

*I had to find my power outside of my organization in terms of mentorship and my culturally proficient journey.*

—White female principal

We have much more to say about educational leadership mentoring. We continue with this important topic in Chapter 6 because we believe that the scarcity of such critical opportunities for women leaders has historically sustained gender inequities in the education profession. We need our male colleagues to join us on this journey toward gender equity.

## WHY THIS BOOK, NOW

We wrote this book for women and men educational leaders to confront and close the gender equity gap. This gap sustains the talent crisis that currently denies highly qualified women and women of color opportunities to better serve millions of public school students. We do not *bash* our male colleagues. We intend for this book to encourage male leaders to enlighten, inform, and mentor other male leaders about the importance of having women leaders at the school sites, at the decision-making tables, in the caucus rooms and board rooms, and certainly in the top positions in the district. Mentors can *sponsor* leaders, men and women, who know and understand the importance of multiple perspectives and experiences, who know and understand the inequities faced by many students and their families as reflected in the multiple data sources at schools and districts. Lack of equity and access means some voices are not heard, some experiences are not valued, some people are never seen, and many potential leaders are ignored. Culturally proficient mentors use the lens of equity to recruit, coach and mentor, sponsor, and support equity leaders on their personal and professional journeys.

## ASSUMPTIONS WE HOLD

- Women are fully capable to lead schools, districts, and other organizations.

- Women require the same access to educational leadership pipelines and pathways as men.

- Since men currently dominate education leadership roles, they must use their platforms to advocate for gender equity and equality.

- The public education system was not built on equality and is grounded in negative stereotypes that men take charge and women take care.

- Negative stereotypes limit women as they progress on their leadership journey.

- Gender stereotypes influence girls and women early in their lives; they feed negative self-images and limit confidence toward taking leadership roles.

- The educational system can be fixed and the lens of Cultural Proficiency is one approach through which women and men can work collaboratively toward gender equity to provide a more inclusive educational environment for female and male students.

## DEFINITIONS WE USE

As coauthors, we are convinced that confusion exists about using the two words *equality* and *equity*. We want our readers to know that without equitable educational practice in schools, equality is not achievable. With gender equity will come gender equality.

To ensure gender equity and eventually equality, which together means fairness of treatment for all students, districts must implement measures, programs, and strategies to compensate for the social and historical disadvantages women faced and still are subjected to in everyday life. And we must all be attentive to ensure that the opportunities presented in everyday life are not limited simply on the basis of gender. In order to have gender equity, educational leaders, policy makers, and lawmakers must change the narrative and turn the focus away from fixing women and focus on the real issue: fixing the system. The current system has suppressed women's opportunities at all levels. As equity advocates and warriors, we acknowledge and will confront systemic oppression for women and people of color in our school districts.

We also acknowledge our awareness and understanding that female–male is a binary conceptualization and recognize there is a nonbinary spectrum of gender identities not limited to male or female identities. Throughout this book, we use a variety of terms to support your learning about equity gaps, lack of access and opportunities, and creation of pathways for gender equity. The following terms are defined using the lens of Cultural Proficiency:

*Woman/Women/Female:* The coauthors intentionally begin our list for terms with these three words. We are aware that the historical use of these terms has been perceived to mean *White* woman/women/female. With this in mind, the authors seek to clarify that when we use these terms we mean *ALL* women. We also use the words *woman/women* and *female(s)* interchangeably through the book. We use the term *women of color* (WOC), specifically, when referring to other than White females. Although we use the terms *female* and *male* throughout the book, we are well aware of the limitations of our language in expressing the vast spectrum of gender identity. At the same time, we wish to acknowledge that the use of such terms is extremely reflective of a very real system of oppression.

*Access:* Opportunities for women leaders to fully participate in and benefit from the educational career ladder and pathways.

*Gender equality:* Viewing men and women as being of equal status and value. Equality is judging people based on their merit and not viewing them as inferior or superior purely based on their gender. Women and men are free to develop their personal abilities and make choices without the limitations imposed by stereotypes and society.

*Gender equity:* The fairness of treatment for men and women according to their respective needs. Equity may include equal treatment or treatment that is different but which is considered equivalent in terms of rights, benefits, obligations, and opportunities.

*Ally:* An individual who is available and present to lend a listening ear *and* use spheres of influence to act on gender inequity issues both in and outside the presence of women.

*Advocate:* An individual who seeks to use personal positional power to intentionally lift up the talents of women leaders and rally for opportunities that allow women to develop the skills needed to be successful in executive positions.

*Mentor:* An experienced, well-seasoned veteran educational leader who imparts knowledge and personal experiences to women leaders who have been identified as candidates for future executive-level positions. Mentors consistently look for conferences and other professional learning opportunities to help position the female mentee for advancement. Mentors often support mentees through high-quality networking in organizations that provide interview skills to prepare female candidates.

*Coach:* One who supports potential women leaders in surfacing consciousness around areas for growth and advancement. Leadership coaches serve to mediate the person being coached from emerging skills to mastering leader skills.

*Sponsor:* One who actively uses positional power to partner with hiring authorities within their networks to advocate for the promotion of women leaders into high-leverage, decision-making positions.

*Pitfalls:* Systems of privilege and entitlement that serve to perpetuate the promotion of males into executive roles when there are female candidates who are more qualified.

*Pipelines:* Explicit platforms designed to ensure that the disproportionality between female and male leaders is eliminated. Opening pipelines for promotions includes the intentional pairing of mentors, sponsors, and coaches with rising women leaders to ensure they move into executive-level leadership roles.

*Pathways:* Opportunities to ensure that women are immersed in diverse experiences and chances that prepare them for executive leadership roles in business operations, curriculum and instruction, technology, human resources, and the superintendency.

*Diversity:* Unique differences among people, including but not limited to gender, ethnicity, sexual orientation, religion, race, age, disability, language, socioeconomic status, physical and mental ability, and cultural background.

*Nonbinary:* Existing or identifying outside the sex/gender binary; gender identity that does not fit the male and female binary. Nonbinary is an umbrella identity, meaning not male or female or not exclusively male or female in gender. Our intention when using *female/woman* and *male/man* is to include the nonbinary aspects of identity.

*Sexism:* Stereotyping, prejudice, or discrimination based on sex or gender, especially against women or girls.

*Benevolent sexism:* A covert and socially accepted form of sexism. A model that refers to positive feelings toward gender role-conforming women and tendencies to protect these women. Patronizing behaviors are perceived as supportive.

*Hostile sexism:* A blatant form of prejudice that centers on antipathy for women, especially those who are nonconforming or challenge the current social hierarchy. Women are viewed as inferior to men.

*Feminist theories:* Overarching perspectives for understanding both the oppression of women in contemporary society and the value held for women and groups who work to confront and overcome injustices grounded in gender. Feminist theories focus on understanding and confronting human behavior and institutional structures, including historical, social, political, and cultural contexts that lead to the oppression of women.

*LGBTQIA+:* An acronym for lesbian, gay, bisexual, transgender, queer/questioning, intersex, asexual/aromantic, and plus for other identities that are not straight and/or not cisgender.

## NOTES TO READERS: YOU AND WE

We use the pronoun *you* to personalize our relationship to the readers of this book. The pronoun *we* refers to the coauthors of this book. We use the pronouns *she* and *he* interchangeably to avoid perpetuating gender misconceptions and the dominance of the longstanding use of the no-longer-neutral, dominant pronoun *he*.

We give gratitude and proper citations to the numerous authors/researchers we have referenced in this book. We have included first and last names for each author in the Reference section to ensure female authors do not go unnoticed or unnamed.

We, the three coauthors, have combined our years of work as educators, school administrators, equity warriors, and scholar practitioners to bring you our experiences, our research, and our best thinking about the importance of responding to the need for gender equity *now* unlike any time in this nation's history. More than ever, the most talented and best-skilled leaders are needed in our schools and districts.

## SHARING OUR NARRATIVE INQUIRY

This book is for women on their education leadership career journeys and the men who support them. We are clear that when we say *support* we are speaking specifically of male educational leaders intentionally and actively doing the following:

- Mentoring women leaders' continuous growth
- Advocating for women to have seats at decision-making tables, on boards, and with their male counterparts
- Allying with and mentoring other men to see the need for having women's perspectives, experiences, and contributions in decision-making roles
- Using the Tools of Cultural Proficiency to lead and conduct a gender equity inquiry and action plan

Current literature is clear: The gender gap and compensation gaps still exist in US public schools. We wanted to hear from female leaders today about their journeys, including the pitfalls along the way, the pipelines available to them, and the pathways they may have chosen. At the Women in Education Leadership Retreat (WELR) we hosted, we asked participants two questions:

1. What were some barriers (pitfalls) that got in your way along your career journey?
2. What were some support factors that helped you overcome those barriers?

We recorded the participants' responses and had the responses transcribed. Selected responses appear in this book as they were transcribed without editing. We do not include names of speakers. The quote is identified by the current leadership role of the speaker.

We also interviewed selected male mentors. We summarized their comments in the text and included some quotes from the male participants.

## THE FORMAT OF THIS BOOK

This book is designed as several things:

- A personal guide for reflecting, planning, and taking action for gender equity
- A discussion guide used with colleagues—in small groups or in large groups
- A book study for developing a school or district Gender Equity Action Plan
- An invitation for you to write your own story. Begin with your SFD (stormy first draft) and let your feelings flow. What happened? Who's involved? Now what?

This book is about *Leading While Female*. We intend to reveal and respond to gender inequities that continue to exist in educational leadership. We emphasize the *inside-out approach* of Cultural Proficiency by designing each chapter to begin with a quote to inspire reflection and motivation for action. The quote is followed by a series of *mirror questions* designed for you to self-assess your values, beliefs, assumptions, and actions. At the end of each chapter, we offer *window questions* for you to examine the policies and practices of your organization related to gender inequities/equity. We have provided lined spaces for you to compose your responses to prompts about the text and suggestions for reflection and action for the *mirror* (inside) questions and *window* (outside) questions. The reflections and the dialogues with your colearners will deepen your learning. Here's a foreshadowing of what's ahead for you:

Chapter 1: Narratives are important. This chapter grounds readers in understanding the impact of *faux* narratives that foster lack of confidence for girls and women. You'll meet the coauthors as we share our stories to support and encourage fellow women to capture their narratives.

Chapter 2: Historical context reminds us that sexism is institutionalized in our schools and continues to foster gender inequities. The Tools of Cultural Proficiency offer women leaders a lens through which to examine barriers to overcome and support functions to locate for career planning.

Chapter 3: Women leaders share their stories of confronting and overcoming barriers to their career development. Women of color describe being targets of implicit bias, as well as other examples of the reactions to systems of oppression within school districts.

Chapter 4: The Guiding Principles of Cultural Proficiency provide a system of core values and assumptions on which female and male leaders can support gender equity in educational leadership. Women's stories highlight the need for identifying systemic support factors.

Chapter 5: This chapter provides an overview of the complexities and differing impact that intersectionality has on the intentional structure of gender inequity. Feminism serves as the umbrella for knowing why and how oppression impacts all women. Therefore, we provide an overview of the evolution of feminist perspectives. We also describe and define the importance of understanding the intersectionality of racism, sexism, and classism and the many identities for female leaders that are perceived differently by some male leaders.

Chapter 6: Women cannot do the work of gender equity alone. We need our male partners. This chapter explores and expands the roles and opportunities for allies, advocates, and mentors.

Chapter 7: Now that we know what we know, to what action are we willing to commit? To ensure gender equity and ultimately gender equality for all women irrespective of barriers we may face, we, the coauthors, hold hope for the future and offer an opportunity for readers to establish a personal and organizational call to *action-for-equity plan* using the Essential Elements for Culturally Proficient Education Practice.

We invite your diverse perspectives, experiences, and expertise that will enhance and expand our learning community. At the end of the book, we offer our email addresses for you to share your stories of barriers you've encountered and support factors you've engaged along the way. We wish you well and join you on your lifelong journey of creating and sustaining culturally proficient educational environments for all educators.

# CHAPTER 1

# Owning the Stories We Tell

## Our Counternarratives

*I know that it takes more than courage to own your own story. We own our stories so we don't spend our lives being defined by them or denying them. And while the journey is long and difficult at times, it is the path to living a more whole-hearted life.*

— Brené Brown (2017, p. 40)

 **LOOKING in the MIRROR**

As you hold the mirror and examine your leadership life, what's the story you own? What might be some descriptors you would use to write or tell the favorite parts of your leadership story? What are your keepsakes and artifacts you would share that best describe you as the main character in your story? To get started with your new narrative, write your responses here as part of your stormy first draft (SFD).

_____

_____

_____

_____

_____

Christina Baldwin (2005) describes *story* as a natural and normal process of how people make sense of life itself. She says, *My story is myself; and I am my story* (p. 21). As coauthors of this book, we wanted to honor stories of women and men educational leaders. To do so, we went in search of educational leaders who aspired to move up the career ladder to provide leadership that would address the inequities in today's classrooms and schools. We interviewed both women and men and asked them to share their stories of support factors and barriers along their journeys. We also collected data from other researchers to write a greater and more complete story of women on their education leadership career journeys. We discovered several patterns and themes that emerged from these data. One theme that surfaced early in our interviews was the theme of *inside-out awareness*: being conscious of values, belief, assumptions, and expectations of individuals, as well as the alignment of vision and mission with policies, practices, and protocols in organizations. We will share additional themes in each of the chapters.

## THE POWER OF STORIES

Brené Brown (2018), a grounded-theory researcher–storyteller, shared a universal truth when she said, *In the absence of data, we will always make up stories* (p. 258). In her ongoing research, she found that neurologist Robert Burton (2008) connects stories with rewarding our brains with dopamine when we define patterns. Stories are certainly patterns: the beginning, setting, characters, conflict, resolution, the ending, and universal themes. Our brains are wired for stories. The brain enjoys clarity, not ambiguity. So if we only have part of a story, our brain has a tendency to make the story complete—not necessarily true, just complete. So, often, we make up what writing teachers call a "stormy first draft" (SFD), as author Anne Lamott (1994) called it in her book *Bird by Bird: Some Instructions on Writing and Life.* Brown's research indicates we often include our fears and insecurities in our SFD. What happens, though, when stories are written about us before we have a chance to write or even imagine our own story? What happens when we let those stories that have been written for us become our stories, even if we haven't had opportunities to write our own story from our hopes and dreams and lived experiences? The *stories that have been written for us* illustrate the power of stereotypes, myths, biases, and low expectations. Let's call those stories "faux stories" or fiction. Some titles of faux stories that already exist include, but are not limited to, the following:

> *The* stories that have been written for us *illustrate the power of stereotypes, myths, biases, and low expectations. Let's call those stories "faux stories" or fiction.*

- *Girls Don't Do Math*
- *Angry Black Women*
- *Girls Build Castles; Boys Build Rockets*
- *Not Many of Us at the Top*

- *College Isn't for You*
- *Latinas: The Quiet Ones*
- *Make a Choice: A Husband or a High-Paying Job*
- *You Talk Funny!*
- *Get Your M.R.S. Degree*
- *You're So Articulate*
- *Once Upon a Time: Not Yet, Though*
- *Girls Are Made of Sugar and Spice and Everything Nice*
- *We Hired a Woman Once*

Just to be clear, we are *not* advocating for young women to become more like stereotypical men: aggressive, dominant, overly strong, and always interrupting. We are asking more male leaders to do these things:

- Embrace the qualities that are often marginalized as feminine.
- Look around the room and see who is there and who is not there and advocate for more women leaders because of the perspectives and experiences they bring.
- Sit back and listen for voices different from their own.
- Question themselves about who they are in relation to their female colleagues. (Menkedick, 2019)

When girls and young women only hear stereotypical and gender-blind stories over and over, they begin to believe the stories are theirs. In the words of Michelle Obama, *It's remarkable how a stereotype functions as an actual trap* (2018, p. 420). As educational leaders, we must write, live, and tell our counternarratives (Yanow, 2011). Our stories portray brave female main characters and compassionate, supportive male characters working collaboratively toward closing the gender equity gap. Our hope in writing our stories parallels Michelle Obama's rationale for writing her story. In her book *Becoming* (2018), former First Lady Michele Obama writes about why she tells her story of becoming who she is today and what she wanted for her daughters:

> It went back to my wishes for them to grow up strong and centered and also unaccommodating to any form of old-school patriarchy. I didn't want them to ever believe that life began when the man of the house arrived home. (p. 207)

She was writing about the need to share with her daughters a different story than the one from her own early years—the same early-years story that was the master narrative for many young girls and women across this nation. She was telling and living a counternarrative, a different story.

## So What's the Current Story?

The data tell a compelling part of today's education leaders' story. Where do educational leaders begin their career journeys? What is the pipeline for school site leaders, assistant principals and principals, and district leaders, assistant superintendents, and superintendents? We know that almost eight in every ten teachers are female, but the number of women in executive leadership roles drops substantially as we look at principals, cabinet-level leaders, and superintendents. Table 1.1, which details the number of women in three leadership roles nationwide, outlines that precipitous drop. Please note that the numbers in the Women of Color column compare to *all* superintendents, regardless of gender. These numbers have been rounded up to represent the best-case number of women per ten individuals in that role. At the state level, the numbers may be lower, as the Chiefs for Change report shows in its state-by-state breakdown (Chiefs for Change [CfC], 2019; Ott, 2019; Robinson, Shakeshaft, Newcomb, & Grogan, 2017; Wyland, 2016).

The current narrative differs only slightly from the mid-1980s and 1990s when women superintendents numbered fewer than three in ten, with fewer than one in ten a woman of color. The story for the past 40 years tells of the overrepresentation of White women as teachers and the underrepresentation of women and women of color in top education leadership positions. So who has been leading our schools and districts? Irrespective of the diverse nature of our preK–12 schools, site- and district-level educational leaders have been, and still are, White men. The career paths for White males are typically by way of middle and high school coaching positions to the principalship to a district office position, then to the top position of superintendent in the same district. However, at the same time his female counterpart starts as an elementary teacher, then becomes a grade-level coordinator, then moves to assistant principal at a middle grades school, then becomes a coordinator or director at the district office, then is an assistant superintendent, and finally becomes superintendent in a different district. The pipeline for women of color is narrower and takes longer (CfC, 2019). This has been a story of unfairness, lack of representation and support, and few opportunities for

**TABLE 1.1** Too Few Women in Leadership Roles: All Women and Women of Color

|  | ALL WOMEN (GENDER ONLY) | WOMEN OF COLOR |
|---|---|---|
| District superintendents | 3 in 10<br>district superintendents are women | 1 in 10<br>is a woman of color |
| Cabinet-level leaders | 6 in 10<br>cabinet-level leaders are women | 3 in 10<br>are women of color |
| Principals | 5 in 10<br>principals are women | 2 in 10<br>are women of color |

SOURCES: Chiefs for Change 2019 report, *Breaking Through: Shattering the Glass Ceiling for Women Leaders* and the National Center of Education Statistics' *National Teacher and Principal Survey, 2015–2016*.

female leaders to move through a system designed for women to teach and men to lead. The true crisis today is that the system is still in place, meaning a loss of talent at the top is squandered.

## Tell New Stories: Change the System

Our intention is to tell stories of women educators who have confronted barriers and are continuing to confront and overcome them today to fill the talent and gender gap created by systemwide inequities. Let's begin by sharing our stories. Each of us, the coauthors, followed a different career path, yet encountered similar barriers along the way to reach our career goals. Together, the three of us span 20 years apart and total almost 50 years of leadership experiences. We placed our stories here in Chapter 1, so you will know who we are and why we are equity warriors.

# OUR STORIES AS COUNTERNARRATIVES

## Trudy's Story: *Your Husband Must Be a Saint*

I grew up in Ventura, a beach town in Southern California. I returned to that beach town to raise my own daughters, and they have returned to that beach town to raise their children. Something about our town calls generations back to the familiarity and the comfort of home, community, sea, and sunsets.

Both of my parents were educators, and although we did not have financial wealth, I knew I was privileged. My family was a well-known family in the community due to my father's winning records on a high school basketball court. He was a legendary coach in a small town, and to this day, 30 years after his passing, I am stopped on the street to be told a story of his influence. I have grown to learn that his influence went far beyond winning seasons as one that impacted the lives of others, mostly young men. My mother spent most of her life taking care of four children and supporting my father on and off the courts. At the age of 97, my mother is the inspiration of our family. Her legacy is living independently for a third of her life, attending book clubs, navigating the Internet, and watching over her four children and all the offspring with unconditional love. I don't believe I have ever heard her say an unkind word to or about anyone, yet she is the strongest and most independent woman I have ever met. It is through her that I have learned not to confuse my greatest strength as a kind, compassionate woman as a weakness.

As siblings, we grew up in a town where we walked to school, played hide-and-go-seek in the streets until dinner was ready, spent hours in and near the ocean, and lived a life with little care. All four of us went on to the university and gained teaching credentials. We are a family of educators.

Throughout my life, I have always sought and been comfortable in leadership positions. From being president of my elementary school to captain of the cheerleading squad in high school, leadership was a place I found satisfaction and value. My memories of K–12 school are positive and validating. I adored many of my teachers, and I knew they adored me . . . an adoration that every child deserves.

## What Led Me to My Why?

I am often asked why I am the way I am. I'm never quite sure what that implies, but I choose to take it as a compliment and an acknowledgment of my quest to ensure equity for every individual. I learned "my why" through experience. I recall in my elementary years when my unwed teacher became pregnant and other families were whispering and speaking unkindly about my beloved teacher. My parents invited her for spaghetti dinner, and five decades later, that teacher, who left the school at the end of that year, writes Christmas cards to my family. I recall the story of my father taking one of his players to the basketball banquet, knowing that the young man's father was an alcoholic and would not be in attendance. Decades later, that young man shared with me that he borrowed my father for one night, and the impact that night had on him resulted in him being a father and grandfather who never missed an event. My father led the canned food drive every year at the high school, and I took over that very drive for 30 years as the organizer in the same district, with the same goal: to ensure every family had a warm meal over the winter break. Being kind to others and extending a hand without judgment were modeled to me through the actions of my parents. I recall my father saying, *Don't tell me who you are; show me what you do and I'll tell you who you are.* I carry this with me in all that I do and all that I am.

## My View of the World

I graduated from high school and decided I needed adventure and freedom. I left for Puebla, Mexico, at the age of 19 and lived in Cholula, Mexico, attending La Universidad De Las Americas. Perfecting my Spanish skills, studying in Mexico, and learning to dance ballet folklorico were all in my plans—meeting my husband was not. Raymundo is a Poblano and was graduating from the university. We were married within the year, and my family embraced him immediately. His family was not so sure about me. His father was hesitant to come to a wedding in California, articulating that he was not certain that a marriage to a White hippie would last. It lasted and resulted in two daughters and two grandchildren. Our bilingual, bicultural parenting was periodically confusing and indicative of our two cultures coming together in what was often foreign territory. Our daughters benefited from the collisions, the duality, and the joy of a bilingual, bicultural home.

## And So It Began

I began my career as a bilingual paraeducator and am forever grateful for the teachers who tapped me on the shoulder and suggested I would be a good teacher. I am easily influenced and proceeded to work toward a bachelor's degree in speech pathology/communicative disorders; eventually, I earned bilingual and special education credentials. This was not easy, as I had a toddler and an infant at the time. My leadership qualities were recognized early on in my career, and I was yet again tapped on the shoulder in the early 1980s. During that time, a female could be dean of girls or possibly an elementary principal. A dean of girls shared with me that she thought I would be a great dean. That was all I needed to be inspired to go to graduate school and earn a master's and administrative credential in educational leadership. After completion, I immediately jumped into a doctoral program at the University of Southern California; I did not tell anyone I was doing this until I ended the first year, as I feared that I was not capable. Fight on! I was immediately hired as an assistant principal at the middle school level.

Two years later, I was promoted to an elementary principal position and enjoyed eight years in a job that I loved. The school was of high poverty, and the children were predominantly Spanish speaking. I recall the superintendent saying that it was the perfect fit for me. In later years, I realized that what was perhaps intended to be a compliment was a statement of earmarking me for my pathway. I noticed that males were the high school principals and the superintendents. I dared to put my name in the hat for a high school principal position after eight years as a successful elementary school principal. I thought it was the job of my dreams.

My dream was not to be realized, and I recall being told that there was much to be done at the school that would take courage and strength. My supervisor likened it to cooking: Although I had most of the ingredients, I did not have them all. I assured him that I could cook. Two years later, I was asked to be the continuation and alternative education high school principal, a place where my skills of "empathy and compassion" could be used. I was officially the first female high school principal in the history of the district—not strong enough to be the principal of a comprehensive high school, yet strong enough to lead those who the system had failed. Again, this was an intended compliment but also a clear indicator of how I was viewed in the organization. The good news is that this short-term, two-year position was one that I would not trade for the world. I learned that the students who need the most deserve the very best, and that was my intention as their principal. After a one-year stint as a director working with student support services, the superintendent announced his retirement. I received the final tap on the shoulder and dared to put my application in for the superintendent position.

## Hometown Girl

I recall my last words in the final interview for the superintendency: *You can search nationwide, but you will never find someone who will love this job like I will.* I left, not knowing if my emotion would be viewed as a strength or a weakness. I was the underdog. The newspaper referred to me as the *hometown girl.* When I was selected as superintendent, I recognized that the

> *It was during the tenure of my superintendency that my gender became very evident. At the first conference I attended, I was redirected to the second floor for the teacher professional development. I had to return to the registration desk and reiterate that I was there for the superintendents' conference. I entered a room with 85% males and was asked if I was the superintendent/principal of a small school district. I proceeded to justify my presence by informing my male colleague that I was the superintendent of a district of 18,000 students. I refrained from a comment when he informed me that he had 3,000 students.*

board of trustees had taken a risk; I was not the logical candidate, and I felt that they had taken a chance on me. I was grateful for their confidence in me and their courage to disrupt history. I was the first female in a role that had historically been filled by a White male. I enjoyed 14 successful years in a job I loved and did my very best to prove to them that they had made the right choice.

It was during the tenure of my superintendency that my gender became very evident. At the first conference I attended, I was redirected to the second floor for the teacher professional development. I had to return to the registration desk and reiterate that I was there for the superintendents' conference. I entered a room with 85% males and was asked if I was the superintendent/principal of a small school district. I proceeded to justify my presence by informing my male colleague that I was the superintendent of a district of 18,000 students. I refrained from a comment when he informed me that he had 3,000 students.

Issues of my gender confronted me throughout the 14 years and have even followed me into my retirement years. During my first year as superintendent, the way I dressed was one of the ratings on the evaluation rubric. I was once told by a colleague that I needed to be "more of a boss," although the giver of that statement could not come up with anything that I had not taken care of within the organization. I was frequently questioned on how I "did it all," with a follow-up statement that my husband must be a "saint." I found myself working twice as hard, running twice as fast, with the goal of proving my leadership and my worth. I turned down two formal raise offers due to my belief that I should not receive a raise if others were not receiving the same.

I recall the time a stakeholder came to see me. The executive assistant was not in her office, so I greeted him, got him coffee, and seated him in my office. His first statement was, *With all due respect, I'd like to meet with the superintendent.* When I informed him that I *was* the superintendent, he shared with me that I was not what he had assumed. I hired the first female for a comprehensive high school and then another. I was asked if I wasn't overdoing the "female leadership thing." I responded that I thought two in the history of the district was still well within the quota. After numerous speeches that dealt with very complex district issues, I was often asked questions such as *Where did you get those shoes? Who cuts your hair?* And, *Oh, have you lost weight?*

As a university instructor and consultant throughout the United States, I hope that my story and my experiences will propel others to put their name in the hat and tap someone on the shoulder. I hope my presence will be a reminder of the work that we have to do in equity and social justice.

My goal is to remain standing and to not be silenced on issues of inequity or bigotry. I had dinner with my eight-year-old grandson recently and shared with him that over the winter break, he got a new superintendent. He looked at me quizzically and asked, *Is she any good?* I smiled and assured him that yes, *he* would be great. I asked him why he assumed it was a she and he said, *Well, Grandma, you were the superintendent and you are a girl.* Our children are watching, and I hope—actually, I expect—that the view will be equitable, honoring, inclusive, respectful, and welcoming.

## Stacie's Story: Don't Believe the Myths

### My Early Years

My journey in K–12 public education can be considered tenuous at best. I entered kindergarten over a decade after the 1954 landmark *Brown v. Board of Education of Topeka* decision, a few years into the Elementary and Secondary Education Act (ESEA) of 1965, and following the assassination of Dr. Martin Luther King Jr. and the enactment of the Civil Rights Act of 1968. These significant, historical time markers are particularly important to me as an African American woman who lived in public housing for the entirety of my elementary and secondary school years. While federal legislation was implemented to ensure that I was provided a quality education, the educational system's barriers prevented me from having the world-class education that many of my White classmates were afforded.

My mother's words are seared into my memory, when she shared with my 14-year-old self that *You will take algebra and chemistry; that is what will get you out of public housing.* Although she didn't graduate from high school, as with many families living in low socioeconomic situations, my mother understood and valued the importance of education. While she couldn't help me with algebra or chemistry, she made certain that I was registered for courses that only two decades earlier I wouldn't have had access to. Do not believe the myth that undereducated parents/families who experience conditions of poverty do not value education. In my case and along my journey, the intersectionality of race and gender has been profound. Barriers to jobs and other opportunities because of my race and gender were hurdles that I needed to overcome. In other words, my race and gender were often viewed by others as deficits rather than assets. In spite of hurdles, I managed to graduate from high school, though not with a stellar academic record; yet, I was the first in my family to earn a high school diploma. That position and accomplishment was something held in high regard in my family. I was also the first family member to attend college.

As a starry-eyed 18-year-old, I entered the northern Minnesota campus with much pride and immaturity. The first weekend I attended a freshman gathering and played a game of pool. As I made my move to win the game with the final eight ball, I heard the voice of a White male student behind me say, *Put that Black bxxxx in there*—I'll leave my thoughts and actions to be deciphered by the reader.

Navigating the unknown terrain of college was difficult for me—difficult as a first-generation college attendee and difficult as a Black student on a predominantly White campus. As Nuri-Robins and Bundy described in their work, I was a *Fish Out of Water* (2016), gasping for oxygen and survival. I didn't fit in at college. Eventually, I succumbed and left school to go to work.

## The Journey

I found that making a living without a college degree was challenging. However, obtaining positions with fairly good wages preempted my return to college for over a decade. Finally, as a wife and parent of three children I found my passion in the service field. I began what would become a 16-year journey in education advancement leadership that would eventually lead to a terminal degree in educational leadership. During this time, I served as a paraprofessional, a teacher, teacher leader, and elementary principal. My mother's hyperfocus on mathematics served me well, as I was a middle school math teacher as well as an elementary school teacher.

At each stage of what I could now call a career, I realized I had the opportunity for a greater impact on students. In addition, at each stage of my career I understood more deeply the profound role that the intersectionality of my race and gender had on my experience as an educator. Prior to the first day of my first teaching assignment, I met with my middle school colleagues. Upon meeting me, one colleague made a statement, followed by two curious questions: *I noticed you are the only math teacher on the team. Did you know that? Are you up for that?* Of course I knew. After all, I had interviewed for the position. I remember that I couldn't help but wonder if she made the comment because I was female in a male-dominated field or if she made the comment because I was African American in a White-dominated field.

I am thankful for the many mentors—both male and female—who served as guideposts and prodders. Dr. Frank Hernandez nudged me to understand that an associate of applied science (AAS) degree and paraprofessional position would allow me to serve students in important, yet limited, ways. Dr. Juanita Hoskins advocated for scholarships for me to complete my bachelor of science in education degree. Florence Odegard and Joe Wemette encouraged me to move into informal leadership roles and formal administrative positions. With their guidance, in ten short years I moved through the educational roles/titles to the principalship.

The principalship brought on new experiences with intersectionality. As a new principal, I stood in the lobby for my first open house both anxious and excited, suddenly feeling the heaviness of the responsibility for ensuring that all 500+ of my students would be immersed in learning experiences that fostered critical thinking and aligned with their passions and ultimately eliminated opportunity gaps. As I greeted students and families, I was approached by a parent who asked, *You're the cafeteria lady right? How do I put money in my son's account?* Working to not show bewilderment, I responded that I was a Jane-of-all-trades but my formal role was that of the school principal, and I introduced her to our cafeteria manager. Again, I left that interaction wondering if it was my gender and my finely pressed skirt and blouse that caused her to think that I was the cafeteria manager, or was it a pervasive mental model that is held for elementary school principals— that is, they *aren't* women of color—that fostered that interaction.

I was often challenged on the decisions I was making. Although I worked to engage stakeholders in many unique and innovative ways, it was assumed that the decisions were unilateral. I heard about my emotional nature and the perception of how my actions were aggressive. I constantly wondered if these comments and questions were because I was supposed to be a demure female leader, or was I being seen as an angry Black woman? Both responses speak to how dynamic the impact of sexism and racism can be. Being a member of both cultural groups simultaneously (intersectionality) can lead a person to question her abilities and then code switch to a point to "get by" in the dominant culture, to the extent that she loses herself and her authenticity. Fortunately, the microaggressions directed toward me served as fuel to forge on in my quest to ensure that historically marginalized students— especially females of color—would be served to the level that the ESEA of 1965 had intended.

## Path of Persistence

Today as I reflect on my experiences and my journey, and although the microaggressions are myriad, I see myself emerging as an educational leader because of my assets as an African American woman. I know, however, that others have perceived those assets as deficits to be overcome. Rather, I've had to overcome the barriers of a system of oppression and entitlement comprised of some people who resist change because they see no need to adapt. The irony is that the core aspects of who I am as a person that have been questioned or seen through a deficit lens are also the very aspects that have helped guide my moral compass as an educational leader and support positive school and district improvement planning and transformation. For instance, due to my background with financial limitations, I know that a parent's care for education and desire for her or his children to succeed has no correlation to the money in their pocketbook, checking, or savings account. As a leader, I accept no excuses when children living in homes with lesser means aren't learning at high levels. My experiences growing up in the

African American community fostered a collectivist nature that serves to bring on partnerships and truly listen to the voice of the marginalized or find and respond to the absent narrative.

As in my grandmother, restoration is deeply embedded in my spirit. See, like my ancestors I seek ways to heal the hurt bestowed on so many through oppression, pushing through the barriers that were placed in front of me—not for self-fulfillment, but for those who will come after. My story, who I am, the destiny my God formed for me is still unveiling itself. While I have many more children and families to serve and many more aspects of myself to discover, what I do know for certain is that Black women have always been resilient restorers, innovators, and visionaries. I am resilient, a restorer, an innovator, and a visionary—all characteristics that leaders in today's educational system must have to solve the complex problems of the 21st century.

## Delores's Story: Magnolias, Sweet Tea, Avocados, and Kale

I am a Southern White woman. I'm proud that I grew up in a small, rural area of northern Mississippi. My daddy taught me to *respect everyone*. He and my mother demonstrated that mantra in their daily lives. The reality was that we lived in a small town with mostly White people. I attended school with only White classmates and had only White teachers until I became a teacher myself in 1969. I did not experience cultural diversity until I was a teacher in Baton Rouge, Louisiana, during court-ordered desegregation. I had read about racism and sexism, but to my knowledge had not experienced either.

I attended elementary, junior high school, high school, and junior college (two years) in the same town—Fulton, Mississippi. My father, one of 12 children, had completed college after WWII with help of the GI Bill. He was the executive office manager for the Itawamba County Office of the US Department of Agriculture. My mother, one of nine children, dropped out of school during her eighth grade year to work and help raise younger siblings. She was one of the brightest people I have known. She was self-educated and had developed an extensive vocabulary as a voracious reader and an avid crossword puzzler.

My parents were strong advocates of public education and insisted my three siblings and I continue our schooling beyond high school. My older brother continued his study of photography in the US Navy, and my two sisters and I became teachers. My brother, sisters, and I attended our elementary, middle, and high school years in classrooms with classmates and teachers who looked just like us: White. Thankfully, our parents taught us to respect everyone and value education.

### Race and Gender in My Early Career Years

Following two years of junior (community) college and deciding to get my bachelor's degree in education to become a teacher, I left the small town of Fulton. I had married a young man who was an outstanding basketball player and wanted to be a teacher and coach. He received a sports scholarship to a small, liberal arts college near Jackson, Mississippi, where we attended together. Once again, I was taught by White instructors and attended classes with only White classmates. Following our graduation, my husband was recruited to coach and teach in East Baton Rouge Parish Schools in Baton Rouge, Louisiana. We moved to Baton Rouge in the late summer of 1968, directly in the midst of court-ordered desegregation of schools.

My husband was assigned his school immediately because of the coaching position for which he had been recruited; however, I was not assigned a school until two weeks before the opening of school. As I look back, I think maybe they knew they "had me" already and could wait until the last minute to appoint me to a school. I anxiously awaited my school designation.

One week before school began, I found out I was pregnant. My husband and I were both surprised and equally excited! I was advised by a teacher friend to meet with my principal immediately and tell him about my pregnancy since that was "policy." I arranged the meeting and was shocked when the principal said to me, *Since, obviously, you conceived prior to your contract date, you will have to resign your position.* He then proceeded to show me the section in the teachers' handbook about conception and pregnancy. I went home in tears and wrote my letter of resignation. I received a call from the school secretary the next day, telling me that the principal invited me to return to the school office and fill out paperwork to become a full-time substitute (no insurance benefits). I returned to the school the following day and submitted my letter of resignation and my application for substitute teaching at the same time. The principal greeted me and said, *I'm glad this is going to work out for you. I received a call from your husband's principal yesterday afternoon. He says your husband is a great guy. We'll do the best we can for you here.*

I learned two weeks later that the principal had another teacher in mind that he preferred hiring full-time rather than me. As I reflect on that conversation, I realize the implications of gender on my assignment and the request for my resignation.

I reported to the high school every day and worked as a substitute teacher, regardless of the subject matter, for four months. One day, I wore a "maternity dress," as we called them back then. The principal called me to his office that morning and thanked me for my "excellent teaching." He also said since I was "showing" I couldn't teach at the high school any longer. To say I was shocked is an understatement. He said I would not be a good role model for the female students. Then, he gave me phone numbers of the nearby middle school and elementary school principals. *They might hire you at their schools because of the younger kids*, he said. They did. I taught at both schools until three weeks prior to our son's birth.

Of course, this story took place in 1968–1969, and we would not think that such gender discrimination could take place today. I recall that things were different for women teachers then. I noticed there were few women and fewer women of color administrators, especially at the secondary level. I noticed that my female colleagues were hesitant to get their master's degree in administration and leadership. I noticed White men were the decision-makers and leaders in education, both locally and nationally. I realized that having women in educational leadership was actually a civil rights issue.

## Career Planning

I taught for six years as a high school English teacher and realized I wanted to be a secondary-level administrator. I chose to attend Southern University (SU) in Scotlandville, Louisiana, to earn my administrative credential and master's degree. SU is a historically Black college and university (HBCU). At the time I attended SU, I was the only White student in the program. One of my African American colleagues recommended I attend SU because she felt I "had a way with Black kids." The experience at Southern University as *the only* White person in the classes changed my life in a powerful, positive direction. While I thought I would learn things at SU that would help me improve my work with Black students, I actually learned more about myself in relation to Black students. Those discoveries led to tension and controversy within my immediate family and among my close friends. Fellow White teachers began to question why I chose *that school* instead of the more popular LSU (Louisiana State University). Family members wondered aloud if I would be safe on the SU campus. Friends seemed confused that I was excited about attending a Black school. I was confused that they questioned my choice.

> *I began to see the difference that being different can make in personal and professional lives. Since those early years of teaching, my work has been focused on equity and inclusion for all students. Because of that focus, somehow I have been able to see the impact that systemic oppression has had on people of color and the impact that privilege and entitlement has had on White people.*

I began to see the difference that being different can make in personal and professional lives. Since those early years of teaching, my work has been focused on equity and inclusion for all students. Because of that focus, somehow I have been able to see the impact that systemic oppression has had on people of color and the impact that privilege and entitlement has had on White people. My experiences at Southern University and serving four years on the district's Desegregation Task Force helped shape my thinking also. I realize I examine personal and professional experiences through my heritage lens and through what might be viewed as racism and hate as well as privilege and entitlement.

My career as secondary teacher, site administrator, central office administrator, and university professor has provided me opportunities to learn about who I am as an individual and an educator. Clearly, my identity is that of an educator for equity and access. I am who I am today because of my life experiences and my educational endeavors. I know that I have benefited from a predominately White educational system because I am a White woman. I also know I've worked very hard to overcome barriers of sexism and a general resistance to change from status quo leadership styles to a visionary, collaborative, equitable leadership style. One of the benefits I experienced from being White was "knowing" the dominant system and having colleagues and mentors who were White men. Sadly, I realized I was supported as the "best" candidate rather than African American females because they were "quota" applicants.

I encountered barriers of sexism when I was told that the assistant principal position I applied for was *really designed for a man because he'll be the last one on campus in the evenings. He'll be the one to lock up everything at night. I [as a male principal] just couldn't ask a woman to do that and still be a gentleman.*

I was once advised by a female senior administrator to *drop that Southern drawl if you want to advance as an administrator in this district. It sounds so put-on and too cute. Men might like it, but I don't.* I replied to her by saying my way of talking was not artificial and was a part of me. I asked for a letter of recommendation, which I received, and took a position in a different district where my Southern drawl was appreciated and respected.

And today, I continue to learn about who I am. As I was teaching in a doctoral program, one of our students talked about his experiences as a Gay man in a leadership role at the local university. Class members engaged in asking questions and commenting on their sexual orientation experiences as well. At one point, I told the story of my teen experience at summer camp. Then I said, *For some Gay people, their lifestyle may seem to not be normal because of the way heterosexual people behave toward them.* Our Gay student turned to me and confidently said, *Dr. Lindsey, for Gay people this is not our lifestyle; this is our life.* I realized that I was using a culturally destructive term and was totally unaware of the impact the word *lifestyle* had on others.

### Lifelong Learner

I continue to learn about myself in relation to others. I've been doing "coffee research" recently to illustrate my point of sexism going unnoticed. My husband and I are both coffee drinkers. When we go to breakfast restaurants, he doesn't drink coffee until after his meal. I observed that when my husband and I are in restaurants together, I have to ask for my first cup because he keeps his cup turned upside down. Also, he is typically asked first when he wants coffee refills, while I've been waiting for my second cup for what seems like forever. So are these small things for me to notice in this crazy world of critical issues? Well, yes, and this informal coffee study serves as a metaphor for invisibility. These are my findings:

- My assumption about women being invisible in the presence of some men is accurate.

- Some people (servers, male and female) are well-meaning people and are unaware of the need to adapt their behaviors.

My husband, a White male and also an equity educator, put it this way:

*I didn't notice because I don't have to. I'm served well by the dominant system. You noticed because you always have to wait. That's the power of sexism. In this case, sexism is oppression expressed as marginalization or microaggression in ways so subtle that usually well-informed people don't notice the slights, whether intended or not, until brought to their attention. Once made aware, the patterns become so obvious as to now be embarrassing that I didn't notice them until pointed out to me.*

Clearly, we all have work to do.

### Final Thoughts

This is not the end of my story, just a pause. These are my final thoughts, as of today. I carefully chose the words for the title of this writing. I still enjoy the fragrance and memories of *magnolias*. I no longer drink *sweet tea*, but I continue to enjoy iced tea without sugar. I've added California *avocados* and *kale* to my plate to help me stay healthy. These words represent the evolution and growth in my life and in my work. I'm clear about who I am as a Southern White woman and as an equity educator. My growth is focused on the question, *Am I who I say I am?* I continue to surface my assumptions about who can teach all learners. The kinds of questions I pose to educators include these: Do we ask some students and their parents to leave part of who they are at the entrance to the school? Do we ask them to "correct their English'" before they give another oral presentation if they sound too "substandard" or too "Southern" or too "Mexican" or too "foreign"?

At what point do we determine what's best for our students or what's best for the school? Whose cultures do we value and celebrate while at the same time dishonoring and devaluing others because they are not American enough?

So here I am, at the end of this writing, but not the end of my story. My children and grandchildren and great-grandchildren will continue my story.

They will lead their lives to reflect the values of equity and social justice that they encounter. Truly, because of them and their colleagues and classmates, I continue to do this work.

Reflecting on our three stories, we value the opportunity to share our journeys in ways that you will reflect on your journey. The following chapters offer you the Tools of Cultural Proficiency as a lens to help examine your values, beliefs, and behaviors related to inequities and gaps that continue to exist in our schools and districts. We offer descriptions of barriers that interrupt gender equity progress and career goals. We explore support factors that our female colleagues shared with us. We offer *feminism*, *sexism*, and *intersectionality* as ways of assessing and understanding our cultural knowledge as women leaders. We use these three terms to respond to the need for more female leaders to bring their skills and talents to executive leadership roles. We encourage our male colleagues to join us on this equity journey. And finally, we propose a template for planning and taking action. Continue with us on this journey for shaping new, refreshing alternative narratives.

 ## Looking Through the Window

As you think about an organization for which you worked or currently work, what is the master narrative of gender equity or inequity for the organization? Who are the main characters? What are some issues that drive conflict? In what ways do gender inequities surface as issues to be confronted? What might be some narratives that already existed prior to your arrival? What might be some narratives that have been identified as counternarratives?

_____

_____

_____

_____

_____

# CHAPTER 2

# Cultural Proficiency

## A Framework for Gender Equity

*Gender equity lifts everyone.*

—Melinda Gates (2019, p. 26)

## LOOKING in the MIRROR

As you look at yourself in the mirror, think about who you are. How comfortable are you in your current workspace and workplace? In what ways might you describe the diversity of the place you spend most of your work time? What happens when you speak up or speak out about lack of inclusion anywhere in the school or district? When was the last time you were invited, encouraged, or required to stretch and learn more about other cultures or groups of people in your work community? Reread the quote by Melinda Gates. What are you learning about yourself when you are stretched beyond your comfort zone?

_____

_____

_____

_____

_____

# A BRIEF HISTORY LESSON ABOUT GENDER INEQUITY

The purpose of this chapter is to provide historical context to gender inequities in the US. Although the contexts of time and places are different today, unfortunately personal stories for women in the workplace have changed little over the past 20 years. Historical and current settings and actions that limited access to leadership opportunities are still part of the current narrative that contributes to the shortage of women educational leaders.

In this chapter, we offer the Tools of Cultural Proficiency as a framework for shifting the conversations from gender inequity to gender equity. The Tools help shift questions about the long-standing inequity of women education leaders from *Why aren't women leaders increasing in numbers?* to *What might be some ways to demonstrate the value of having women leaders in top positions in schools and districts?*

Inclusion-focused women and men who are leading our schools and school districts to the highest levels of educator effectiveness and student achievement seem to have clear understandings and visions of equity. These leaders also take responsibility to learn and understand historical social inequities to better determine the educational inequities that might exist in individual educators' practices and organizational policies and procedures. District and site leaders who are committed to their personal journeys in understanding their values, beliefs, and assumptions are well prepared to inquire about the inequities that may exist in their school or school district's policy development and implementation of educational practices.

## Looking Back, Moving Forward

When educational leaders understand historical context of the *-isms*, their choices for becoming equitable educators are clear and intentional (Lindsey, Roberts, & CampbellJones, 2013). Discovering and exposing inequities must be the critical first steps in devising equitable educational practices. However, when confronted with the data some educators reject considering historical inequities as being perpetuated by dominant White educators who have allowed these unfortunate circumstances to persist. Rather than responding with anger or defensiveness, we must realize that although we educators today didn't cause the inequities, the historical, societal, and educational forces delivered these inequities to our doorsteps to be addressed now (Lindsey, 2018).

> *Discovering and exposing inequities must be the critical first steps in devising equitable educational practices.*

Discussions of how our country's heritage favored straight, property-owning White men over women and how those inequities (sexism) continue to affect today's schooling are often met with disbelief and dismissed with comments such as, *Women just can't lead like men do.* The fact remains that inequity for women, people of color, and non-property-owning men was codified into the US Constitution when only property-owning White males were guaranteed rights in that document. However, women, people of color, and First Nations people were working and participating in the nation's growth as if they were invisible. Lindsey (2018) describes these early conditions in *The Cultural Proficiency Manifesto: Finding Clarity Amidst the Noise*:

> *Parallel and often overlapping gender and racial discrimination existed together with social stratification in which low-income White men were marginalized from being full-fledged members of society. White men had more social mobility than women or people of color but also knew their "place" or role in society. An advantage they inherited, in most cases, was not being on the lowest rung of the socioeconomic ladder. In fact, during the European migrations of the late 18th and throughout the 19th centuries European migrants to our shores often stepped up into an emerging middle class due to their advantage of being White and being able to participate in the political and economic functions of society. The opportunity to ascend into the middle class does not detract from their hard work, sacrifices, or accomplishments. The distinction is no matter how hard women, indigenous, and people of color strive, doors were shut or, at best, opened only slightly.* (p. 23)

The signers of the US Constitution were wise and forward thinking in including the amendment process. Throughout our nation's historical struggles for rights for all citizens, women, people of color, and sometimes their White male allies worked together to change the social contract. Everyday people and well-known personalities have used legal, political, and economic avenues to push for changes in the nation. As a result of these efforts, the abolitionist movement surfaced in the late 18th century, the well-organized women's suffrage movement was formalized in the mid-19th century, and the civil rights movement pushed forward throughout the mid- to late 20th century. The 21st century continued with approval of same-sex marriage and the #MeToo movement. However, these movements and forces are being met with engrained resistance that continues even today. Although women, especially women of color, are more present than ten years ago in boardrooms, on executive leadership teams, and even in the superintendent's chair, they continue to have their comments interrupted by male leaders, to be ignored for promotions, and to stand invisible as decision-makers and problem solvers. Without a clear foundation or framework of action for gender equity, our schools and community partners will miss experiencing the valuable contributions of women leaders. We offer Cultural Proficiency as the Framework to guide the inclusion of female leaders in all aspects of schooling.

## A Framework for Equity, Access, and Inclusion for Women Leaders

Equity action plans, typically required for schools and districts to receive federal or state funding, cannot be fully developed without identifying previously unrecognized or unacknowledged inequities in classrooms or schools.

Cultural Proficiency is a conceptual framework for ensuring equitable opportunities, access, and inclusion for all demographic groups into an educational environment. The Tools of Cultural Proficiency provide processes

> *that can be used by both historically dominated and dominant group members to replace myths and stereotypes with the images, information, and skills that equip them to have substantive dialogue that results in equitable actions within schools.* (Cross, Bazron, Dennis, & Isaacs, 1989; Tappan, 2006, as quoted in Lindsey, Nuri-Robins, Terrell, & Lindsey, 2019, p. 77)

## APPLYING THE CULTURAL PROFICIENCY CONCEPTUAL FRAMEWORK

Senge et al. (2000) used the term *mental model* in much the way we use the term *conceptual framework*. Simply put, a conceptual framework is a pictorial representation of one's thoughts, values, actions, policies, and practices. In this case, the conceptual framework is akin to a road map in that it allows sojourners for social justice to determine where they are on the journey to Cultural Proficiency and to develop plans for getting to where they want to be.

The Tools of Cultural Proficiency are as follows:

- **The Barriers:** Social constructs that function as negative core values that, when understood, guide overcoming resistance to equity

- **The Guiding Principles:** Underlying positive core values of the equity approach

- **The Continuum:** Language that describes both healthy and non-productive policies, practices, and individual values and behaviors

- **The Essential Elements:** Behavioral standards for measuring, and planning for, growth toward cultural proficiency

Table 2.1 shows the Tools and the manner in which they interact with and inform one another. The interaction and interrelatedness of the Tools elevate them from being separate and discrete to being a conceptual framework for how educators improve practice. Take a closer look at Table 2.1 and use the following section as a guide.

### Guidance in Reading Table 2.1

First, read the table from bottom to top. You may find these prompts helpful:

- At the bottom of the table, notice the manner in which the arrow flowing from the Barriers to Cultural Proficiency informs the left side of the Continuum, fostering practices that are culturally destructive, incapacitating, and blind.

**TABLE 2.1**  The Conceptual Framework for Culturally Proficient Practices

**The Five Essential Elements of Cultural Competence**

*Serve as standards for personal, professional values and behaviors, as well as organizational policies and practices:*

- Assessing cultural knowledge
- Valuing diversity
- Managing the dynamics of difference
- Adapting to diversity
- Institutionalizing cultural knowledge

*Informs*

**The Cultural Proficiency Continuum portrays people and organizations who possess the knowledge, skills, and moral bearing to distinguish among healthy and unhealthy practices as represented by different worldviews:**

| *Unhealthy Practices* | | *Healthy Practices* |
|---|---|---|
| • Cultural Destructiveness | Differing | • Cultural Precompetence |
| • Cultural Incapacity | Worldviews | • Cultural Competence |
| • Cultural Blindness | | • Cultural Proficiency |

*Informs*

*Informs*

**Resolving the tension to do what is socially just within our diverse society leads people and organizations to view selves in terms unhealthy and healthy.**

| **Barriers to Cultural Proficiency** | E | **Guiding Principles of Cultural Proficiency** |
|---|---|---|
| *Serve as personal, professional, and institutional impediments to moral and just service to a diverse society by doing the following:* | t h i c a l | *Provide a moral framework for conducting one's self and organization in an ethical fashion by believing the following:* |

Barriers to Cultural Proficiency

*Serve as personal, professional, and institutional impediments to moral and just service to a diverse society by doing the following:*

- Being resistant to change
- Being unaware of the need to adapt
- Not acknowledging systemic oppression
- Benefiting from a sense of privilege and entitlement

E
t
h
i
c
a
l

T
e
n
s
i
o
n

Guiding Principles of Cultural Proficiency

*Provide a moral framework for conducting one's self and organization in an ethical fashion by believing the following:*

- Culture is a predominant force in society.
- People have individual and group identities.
- Diversity within cultures is vast and significant.
- Each cultural group has unique cultural needs.
- The best of both worlds enhances the capacity of all.
- The family, as defined by each culture, is the primary system of support in the education of children.
- School systems must recognize that marginalized populations have to be at least bicultural and that this status creates a distinct set of issues to which the system must be equipped to respond.
- Inherent in cross-cultural interactions are dynamics that must be acknowledged, adjusted to, and accepted.

- Notice how the arrow flowing from the Guiding Principles of Cultural Proficiency informs the right side of the Continuum, leading to practices that are culturally precompetent, competent, and proficient. In effect, adherence to the Guiding Principles as asset-based core values will enable people and organizations to overcome Barriers to Cultural Proficiency.

- On the right side of the Continuum, the Five Essential Elements serve as standards for educator and school practices, enabling cross-cultural effectiveness.

The Tools of Cultural Proficiency equip individual educators and their schools with the agency to make meaningful, intentional changes that benefit all students.

## Sexism Is Systemic

The Tools of Cultural Proficiency provide an equity lens for examining the work of female and male educational leaders within the educational environments they work. It's no secret that our country has a history of gender discrimination and sexism. And the disparities of valuing males above females are still evident in classrooms across the nation. For example, researchers MacNell, Driscoll, and Hunt (2015) used an online college class divided into four discussion groups to study gender bias. The four groups were then divided evenly between two course instructors. One instructor was male, and the other instructor was female. The two instructors shared his or her correct gender to one group and the opposite to the other group. At the end of the course, students submitted final evaluations of their instructors. The results showed that students rated the instructors they thought were male much higher than the professors believed to be female, regardless of the professor's actual gender. The instructor that students thought was a man received markedly higher ratings on professionalism, fairness, respectfulness, giving praise, enthusiasm, and promptness. The researchers of the study concluded this:

> *Our findings show that the bias we saw here is not a result of gendered behavior on the part of the instructors, but of actual bias on the part of the students. Regardless of actual gender or performance, students rated the perceived female instructor significantly more harshly than the perceived male instructor, which suggests that a female instructor would have to work harder than a male to receive comparable ratings. If female professors and instructors are continually receiving lower evaluations from their students for no other reason than that they are women, then this particular form of inequality needs to be taken into consideration as women apply for academic jobs and come up for promotion and review.* (MacNell, Driscoll, & Hunt, 2015, p. 11)

The researchers plan to continue this study to examine themes and patterns for gender preferences as online instructors.

Dr. Erin Davis, a gender studies professor at Cornell College, identified the underlying problem of gender disparities through instructor evaluations of men and women as using different traits or having different expectations for individuals who are doing the same job. Davis notes, *On campus, a professor's ability to nurture or mentor a student is certainly valued, but intellectual ability is generally the more prized quality in a professor* (Huntsberry, 2015, para. 5). Dr. Benjamin M. Schmidt, using the website Rate My Professor, confirmed the same hypothesis as Dr. Davis. Schmidt, an assistant professor of history at Northeastern University and a faculty member in the NuLab for Texts, Maps and Networks, created a database based on the words used in 14 million reviews (Jaschik, 2015). The word choices entered by students reveal, by discipline, how common the words were (per million words of text) in reviews. The findings show the differences by gender of the faculty member. The same data was also sorted strictly for positive and negative reviews or for all reviews. Dr. Schmidt reported words most often associated with men included *smart, cool, interesting, genius, corny,* and *boring*. Words most often used to describe women were *sweet, shrill, warm, strict, organized, frumpy,* and *cold*. Schmidt concluded that students who posted responses tend to rate professors on two different scales: intelligence for men, nurturing for women (Fugler, 2015; Jaschik, 2015).

So an obvious response to the question *How do we fix these disparities and unbalanced views of women and men* might be, *Hire more women as educational leaders*. Educational institutions from preK–12 through postsecondary are the most promising arenas for change because future generations of employees and eventual employers spend time in school environments. As members of the education community, we have the opportunity to change minds and hearts about who leads most often, better, faster, and differently.

## SLOW GROWTH

Despite a steady growth in female representation in the roles of teacher and principal, female representation in the superintendency has seen little increase in the past few decades. Change is taking longer than we had hoped (Ott, 2019; Wallace, 2014). In 2008, the USDOE (US Department of Education) reported that using an annual rate of .7% increase, it would take 77 years for females to be proportionately represented in the superintendency (Wallace, 2014). Dr. Maria Ott, a former superintendent, using self-reported data from the American Association of School Administrators (AASA), supports the slow, yet consistent rate of increase of women and women of color educational leaders (Ott, 2019). Table 2.2 displays the data showing the rate of change.

**TABLE 2.2**  Increase of Female Superintendents in the US, 2000–2019

| YEAR | FEMALE SUPERINTENDENTS | FEMALES OF COLOR AS SUPERINTENDENTS |
|------|------------------------|--------------------------------------|
| 2000 | 14% | 4% |
| 2019 | 24% | 6% |

SOURCE: Ott, 2019, and Wallace, 2014.

Table 2.2 represents the first decade of the 21st century's overall increase of women in the workplace. Also, these data reveal the slow pace (less than 1% a year) for women as top decision-makers and vision setters in our nation's schools. Certainly, we can expedite this slow rate, and it starts with a shift in conversation about educational leadership. In her study of the disproportionality of female superintendents to male superintendents, Teresa Wallace (2014) identified four challenges/barriers that men rarely encounter:

- Taking longer career paths to the superintendency than men
- Working under pressure to balance family and work life more than men
- Finding qualified and supportive female mentors who have overcome barriers
- Matching female candidates to districts that no longer hold gender bias and stereotypical behaviors against female leaders

We propose that successful women leaders who share their stories of overcoming barriers will actually change the job itself through collaborative practices and shift the conversation. Female leaders mentoring aspiring female leaders will help change perceptions of women as "less than men" and more as successful peers.

Disparities and differences in how women are treated in a male-dominated district leadership work environment may influence how women continue to be treated, no matter who she is. Consider the story of a husband–wife team of superintendents. They were interviewed at different times during a local networking event. On their drive home, the female superintendent said, *I'm always asked that annoying question, "How do you balance work and family?"* Her husband replied, *"Hmmm, no one has ever asked me that question."*

Cultural Proficiency helps us shift the conversation from being stuck in negative stereotypes for women and men educational leaders. The Cultural Proficiency Framework and interrelatedness of the Tools that comprise the Framework provide a way to examine gender inequity in educational leadership. Cultural Proficiency is a personal journey for an educational leader to closely examine his or her values, beliefs, and assumptions about who teaches, who leads, and who learns. This personal exploration reveals biases and prejudices typically grounded in personal, cultural, and professional experiences since, generally speaking, we all have conscious and unconscious biases. Reflective practice, dialogue, and interaction with people who are different from ourselves will help surface our views of our students, their families, and the communities we serve. Additionally, a culturally proficient educational leader works within the school district to intentionally examine policies, practices, procedures, handbooks, rulebooks, and other guideline documents relative to the cultural or demographic groups served by the district. The personal exploration of values, beliefs, and assumptions and the intentional review of policies and practices are referred to as the *inside-out process* of culturally proficient educational practice.

## THE TOOLS PROVIDE A FRAME OF REFERENCE FOR ACTION

### Tool: Barriers to Cultural Proficiency

Barriers to Cultural Proficiency that continue to get in the way of gender equity are both individually and institutionally constructed. Recall from the previous chapter that even though more teachers are women, they occupy fewer and fewer positions in education leadership the higher up we look in the organizational structure so that only three in ten superintendents are female (Maranto, Carroll, Cheng, & Teodoro, 2018). Throughout current research and in our interviews with female educational leaders, we found stories of women acknowledging and overcoming barriers. We also found that women are twice as likely as men to have served as curricular leaders and coordinators (31.3% of women and 16% of men), while men were three times as likely (52.8% of men and 16.5% of women) to have served as athletic coaches. Overall, men are proportionately more likely to gain promotion to principal and to do so more quickly than women. In traditional public schools, male principals have taught a mean of only 10.7 years before becoming principal, compared to 13.2 years for women (Maranto et al., 2018). Today, district leaders must be willing to look beyond the traditional résumé-building experience and provide equitable candidate support for women with appropriate skills and talents for movement along and up the career ladder without encountering barriers of sexism (e.g., men are better at leadership).

As coauthors, we determined that individual and institutional barriers that women educational leaders face can be categorized as the following:

- Being unaware of the school or district's need to adapt to having White and women of color leaders at all levels

- Denying the existence of sexism and gender inequities as systemic oppression

- Denying the existence of systemic privilege and entitlement that favors male leaders

- Resisting change that aids in attracting, recruiting, and mentoring women (White and women of color) in leadership positions

Crystal Morey, a K–6 instructional coach in Kent, Washington, is an educational blogger. Crystal spent the past seven years teaching middle-level mathematics. She told the story of believing her parents when they said she could be anything she wanted to be. However, early in life she experienced defeat in a class election by the "golden boy" in school. Later in life, she continued to experience gender inequities. In one of her blog posts, Morey (2017) wrote,

> Unfortunately, the data confirms what, in my heart, I've already observed in my professional journey . . . [W]hile 75% of the educational field is composed of women, only 30% of educational leadership roles are held by women. This discrepancy considers many factors, including female to female competition, "Imposter Syndrome," which is described as the inability of high-achieving women to internalize their accomplishments as rightfully deserved, mom-guilt (closest to my own heart), and the like.

> [Another] post that speaks to the disproportionate number of female and male conference speakers at large is "Raising Shakespeare's Sister (Or Why We Need to Talk About Female Speakers in Search)." This piece presents research on the ratings conference goers give to male and female speakers. Female speakers are rated lower (on average) than their male counterparts. Author Hannah Smith concludes, "Success and likeability are positively correlated for men and negatively correlated for women. This means that men who are successful are also considered likeable. However, women who are successful are not considered likeable." (paras. 3–4)

What might be some implications for women education leaders encountering barriers as they pursue roles and goals as speakers and leaders?

## Reflection

What are you noticing about the barriers as default core values? What might be some barriers that are interrupting or delaying your leadership or mentoring journey?

_____

_____

_____

_____

_____

## Tool: The Guiding Principles of Cultural Proficiency

The Guiding Principles of Cultural Proficiency foster the development of a set of core values focused on equity, access, and inclusion. According to Lindsey et al. (2019), these values serve as the following:

- A moral framework for conducting one's self and her or his school and district in an ethical manner

- Guides for who we say we are as leaders

- Guides to determine actions to overcome individual and institutional barriers

- Manifestations of how the school district serves historically marginalized groups

Clearly, the beliefs displayed in the Guiding Principles of Cultural Proficiency were evident among the female participants at the Women in Education Leadership Retreat (WELR) described throughout this book. To successfully overcome barriers, these women rely on their solid core values, their talents and expertise, and the support and encouragement from mentors throughout their careers.

As a historically marginalized group, female educational leaders have unique cultural needs. Overcoming barriers to equity requires women leaders to push through the limitations that have been set upon and in front of them. Perseverance to overcome sometimes emerges through external recognition and nudges, such as those expressed from many of the women leaders at WELR. Some participants spoke about nurturers who saw beyond what participants often thought of themselves; others saw their own capabilities and—through encouragement and support from others—helped set in motion the trajectory of their leadership careers. Leader after leader referred to the "taps on the shoulder" from their principals, HR directors, and professors. Nurturers seem to know that invitations to serve on teacher-leader committees, strategic planning teams, and organizational boards are the seeds that foster women leadership. One retreat participant said,

> [W]e all need that, that someone to help take us by the hand and say you can do this and this is how you do it without losing your job. And I always talk about that. . . . You can be courageous and keep your job.

White female HR consultant leaders also spoke of their support and motivation coming from the members of the school communities in which they served. Through the development of deeper relationships with students and families, they were compelled to *do more*, to form community partnerships, and to advance their educational studies for the specific purpose of building their capacity to better serve members of marginalized groups. A retired Latina female administrator shared that *my life was changing and my lens was changing by immersing myself in the communities where I was working and getting to know families in the way that I did and becoming really vulnerable myself.*

Another leader was compelled to further her education when a young female African American student looked at her and asked, *You're brown and you can be smart too?* The opening of doors for these women leaders also led to the opening of doors for marginalized students and their families (Arriaga & Lindsey, 2016).

Several women leaders shared that once they were set on the pathway to become an educational leader, support from members in professional organizations helped them sustain their careers. Some women spoke of the difference networks made in developing confidence and often serving as the linchpin in securing a position as superintendent, as an African American superintendent shared:

> [It's] *creating a space for yourself to learn and to have not only a statewide network but a national network that has been huge in supporting me. . . . I told my board, "You're not getting one person, you're gaining a nationwide network," and so my superintendency is a collective knowledge base that you're getting.*

We also found in our conversations with many women leaders that professional support took the form of affinity groups helping to address specific identity and cultural needs. Time with other women of color allowed them to share their stories and find support. They enjoy attending conferences for women and specifically women of color.

In our quest to be culturally proficient, we understand that women as a group are not monocultural. As an illustration, one of the Guiding Principles notes that *diversity exists within group identity*; the diversity amongst women leaders is vast, significant, and is often referred to as intersectionality of identity. Women identify by their gender, ethnicity, race, sexual orientation, language, faith, and ableness. Intersectionality is the overlapping structures of subordination in which marginalized people are too often situated. Intersectionality manifests itself in the consequences of interactive oppressions, the elimination of people's experiences at the intersections of multiple oppressions, and the cultural construction of identities that result in negative stereotypes that are used to further discredit marginalized experiences (Agosto & Roland, 2018). One educational leader who is female, Black, and Gay shared that she is all of these identities, experiences, and perspectives.

While the retreat participants appreciated the camaraderie that existed in the all-female leadership cohort, one Latina female superintendent, who is active in community organizations, wanted everyone to understand an important element of gatherings:

*The intentionality around forming the network and forming pro-found relationships also helps you professionally . . . strength comes not from my family only but my professional family. That's how I've met so many people.*

## Reflection

What are you noticing about the Guiding Principles as core values? In what ways might these Guiding Principles support your leadership or mentoring journey?

_____

_____

_____

_____

_____

## Tool: The Continuum

The Continuum is used as an individual (self) and organizational assessment for progress. The Continuum reflects the influence of both the Barriers and the Guiding Principles. The Continuum is used to assess where a member of an organization is as a culturally healthy, knowledgeable, and productive individual, as well as to asses who we are as an organization demonstrated by our policies, practices, and protocols. Using the Continuum helps us closely examine our values, beliefs, and assumptions translated into why we do what we do in our personal lives as well as members of our organizations.

The Continuum

- informs our actions ranging from culturally destructiveness to culturally proficient and
- serves as an assessment for reflection and continuous growth.

The Continuum does not

- imply judgement of individual's behaviors or
- indict or punish individuals for actions.

The six points of the Continuum, using the lens of gender equity, are as follows:

- Cultural Destructiveness: Seeking to eliminate women as leaders.
- Cultural Incapacity: Seeking to make the culture of others, especially women and women and men of color, appear to be wrong. Seeing no need for women leaders.

- Cultural Blindness: Refusing or pretending to acknowledge the culture of others, especially women and women and men of color. Gender blindness ensures traditional, male-dominated educational leadership roles.

- Cultural Precompetence: Being aware of what one doesn't know about working in settings with women as non-formal leaders and as formal, designated leaders. This is the initial level of awareness after which a person/organization can move in positive, constructive direction. Members begin to notice contributions of women leaders.

- Cultural Competence: Viewing one's personal and organizational work as an interactive arrangement in which the educator enters into diverse settings in a manner that is valued and additive to cultures that are different from the educator, especially women and women and men of color. The Five Essential Elements are the standards for action to intentionally move forward with purposeful outcomes for gender equity.

- Cultural Proficiency: Making the commitment to lifelong learning for the purpose of being increasingly effective in serving the educational needs of *all* cultural groups. Cultural Proficiency requires individuals and core leader groups to hold the vision of what can be; then, the members must commit to systemwide monitoring and measuring (benchmarking) for success on the journey to gender equity.

The first three points on the Continuum may find us referring to our students as *under-performing*, or unqualified for roles because of their gender or ethnicity. We've heard these blatant comments made by males:

- *Women really don't know enough about politics to even vote.*

- *Women have too many things to do at home to be considered a serious candidate for principal.*

- *I'm not sure she's smart enough to lead a school. She doesn't even speak English very well.*

- *I can't imagine a woman principal dealing with this faculty or community.*

- *Women are way too emotional to lead at that high level.*

The following comments are blatant and typically spoken by people in the organization who have made their biased views/beliefs about women leaders well known. However, some comments are subtler (though no less offensive):

- *I didn't know you had an interest in leadership, given you've just started your family.*

- *She's too nice. She just doesn't look the type to be a principal.*

- *I never thought you'd ever want to leave the classroom; you're like a mom to these kids.*

These comments can be made with no intention of sexism or harm of any kind. They are statements of unintentional, or unconscious, bias, and the speaker is often unaware what he or she said was offensive. Even so, the effect of the comments still can be hurtful. These statements would be placed at Cultural Blindness on the Continuum.

The next three points on the Continuum reflect our references to the ways in which we are underserving our students and their communities and showing our value for gender equity. We would hear comments such as these:

- *As a White male leader in this district, I can see why women feel undervalued. Now that we've put that on the table as reality, what are we going to do about it?*

- *My daughters can do anything my sons can do—when they are given the opportunity!*

- *Sometimes, rules need to be revised, especially HR rules. Women never get to the interview stage because as men, we men don't consider them qualified. Why is that the case?*

- *The fact that she speaks several languages, was successful as a deputy superintendent, and serves on numerous community boards tells me she can certainly do the work of a superintendent.*

- *I'm so sorry for what I just said. Now that I know the comment offends you, I will not say it again. I now see why you're offended and upset.*

When members of your organization speak about policies, practices, and protocols, what do you hear them say about men, women, and people of color? The Continuum helps us examine our actions and our progress toward Cultural Proficiency and gender equity.

## Reflection

What are you noticing about the Continuum as an assessment tool? What might be some ways you will use this information on your leadership or mentoring journey?

_____

_____

_____

_____

_____

## Tool: The Five Essential Elements

The Five Essential Elements are the actions for equitable leadership behaviors within the communities we serve. The Essential Elements, which follow, are the standards for culturally competent values, behaviors, policies, and practices:

- Assessing Cultural Knowledge
  - Being aware of what you know about others' cultures, about how you react to others' cultures, and what you need to do to be effective in cross-cultural situations.
  - Collecting and analyzing data about gender inequities.
- Valuing Diversity
  - Making the effort to be inclusive of people whose viewpoints and experiences are different from yours. These values will enrich conversations, decision-making, and problem solving.
  - Recognizing the diversity of perspectives and experiences females bring to the district.
- Managing the Dynamics of Difference
  - Viewing conflict as a natural and normal process that has cultural contexts to be recognized and understood.
  - Being supportive in decision-making, creative problem solving, and community building by developing a gender-inclusive environment.
- Adapting to Diversity
  - Having the will to learn about others and the ability to apply others' cultural experiences and backgrounds in educational settings.
  - Acknowledging and demonstrating the changing needs of a community using the lens of gender equity.
- Institutionalizing Cultural Knowledge
  - Making learning about cultural groups and their experiences and perspectives an integral part of continuous growth and learning.
  - Establishing new policies and revising inequitable practices to support gender-inclusive schools and districts.

These five verbs—*assess, value, manage, adapt*, and *institutionalize*—are key actions to implementing districtwide equity plans:

- Step One: Implement an inquiry to collect data about gender inequities and determine outcomes for equity actions.
- Step Two: Analyze the data to determine the depth of the inequities.

- Step Three: Recognize the barriers toward gender equities.

- Step Four: Identify key actions using Essential Elements to overcome barriers.

- Step Five: Determine an assessment plan and monitor progress toward gender equity outcomes for equity actions.

*Reflection*

What are you noticing about the Essential Elements as action verbs? What might be some actions you will take on your leadership or mentoring journey to support gender equity?

_____

_____

_____

_____

_____

## Looking Through the Window

As you look through the window, in what ways are the four Tools of Cultural Proficiency used as a foundation in your organization/district to ensure gender equity? Can you identify specific practices that present themselves as barriers to gender equity? How might leaders focus on opening windows to gender equity? What are networks that support women in leadership in your community? How might the networks/organizations be strengthened to be more inclusive?

_____

_____

_____

_____

_____

# CHAPTER 3

# Confronting and Overcoming Barriers

*We should each be free to develop our own talents, whatever they may be and not held back by artificial barriers, man-made barriers, certainly not heaven sent.*

—Ruth Bader Ginsburg, Supreme Court Justice

 **LOOKING in the MIRROR**

Look in your mirror: Can you recall experiencing or can you identify gender bias as such in your formative years? How have those experiences contributed to who you are as a female educational leader today? To the best of your knowledge, have you ever been denied a position because of your gender or sexual orientation? What were you told was the reason you didn't get the promotion for which you applied? Did you "not apply" because someone advised you not to because of your gender or sexual orientation? What were your thoughts regarding these situations?

_____

_____

_____

_____

_____

## WORDS HOLD *POWER OVER*; FEMALES BRING *POWER WITH*

Have you heard or spoken these words?

- *She's too old to start her leadership career.*
- *She's too aggressive when it comes to personnel matters.*
- *She's too soft/feminine when it comes to decisions.*
- *She wears her heart on her sleeve.*
- *She doesn't work well with other women.*
- *She's not ready yet.*
- *She's too bold and aggressive when she talks.*
- *She never says much in our leadership team meetings. She needs to speak up.*

We asked women in educational leadership roles these questions: *What are some of the barriers that got in the way of your progress on your leadership journey? What might be some support factors you found on your journey?*

Their responses included the following:

- *I had to learn the "good ol' boys" system and who my allies were.*
- *My mentor was a man who mentored other men about the benefit of having women in the organization.*
- *I worked really hard to overcome stereotypical views of women as leaders.*
- *I went to a different district and found leaders who supported equitable and inclusive hiring practices.*
- *I learned how to integrate my home culture with my work culture.*

As we dialogue regarding how far we have come as females or debate if we have "arrived" as educational leaders, we are faced with the fact that only two out of every ten principals and fewer than one in ten district superintendents are women of color, a number that has been left virtually unchanged in the last 26 years. Clearly and consistently, women educational leaders—especially women of color—are underrepresented when comparing the male to female ratio of administrators as opposed to the representation of female to male teachers in classrooms. So as educators, we can continue to accept the status quo, or we can declare these limitations on leadership opportunities are no longer acceptable! We have committed to the latter and are writing this book to step up, stand up, and break through the silence that perpetuates the current educational leader gender imbalance.

## BACK TO OUR BEGINNINGS

As we reflect on the disappointing data regarding female educational leaders, we cannot deny the impact of our experiences, particularly in our formative years that persist into the 21st century. Nursery rhymes and fairy tales depict the boy as Peter Pan—the hero, the protector, and the leader. Girls are provided the model of Wendy—the caretaker, the nurturer, the follower. Nursery rhymes are ever so subtle, yet disturbingly intentional as our children are wooed to sleep with thoughts of little boys being made of snips and snails and puppy dog tails and little girls of sugar and spice and everything nice. Jack Be Nimble is quick, Peter Pumpkin Eater couldn't keep his wife and put her in a pumpkin shell, and Georgie Porgie kissed the girls and made them cry. Yet we recall that Jill followed Jack up the hill, Polly put the kettle on, Little Bo Peep lost her sheep, and Cinderella and Sleeping Beauty were rescued by their Prince Charming.

Simultaneously, as girls become princesses and celebrities, boys are encouraged to become rescuers and super heroes. Boys build Lego structures, explore science, and create new designs. Girls are guided to participate in activities that do not require technical, scientific, or spatial skills and are reminded to be cautious and sit quietly. The consequence of this hidden agenda for girls is that it can instill a sense of inferiority and helplessness in the developing, impressionistic minds of our children—both boys and girls—before they even enter our schools.

When our children enter the K–12 system, gender bias subtleties become less subtle and more pronounced. Think of the symbolism of our kindergarten children being taught to line up by gender and how high school graduates are assigned their graduation robe color by gender. Behavioral expectations reinforce the stereotype that "boys will be boys," which too often continues the oppression of female marginalization throughout their preK–12 school years. Girls are praised for polite, neat, and passive behavior, while boys are encouraged to speak up, be actively engaged, and be innovative. Late 20th century researcher Bailey (1992) reported support for what is often viewed as stereotypical, binary behaviors: *Girls in grades six and seven rate being popular and well liked as more important than being perceived as competent or independent. Boys, on the other hand, are more likely to rate independence and competence as more important* (p. 1).

However, a more recent study conducted by Tan, Oe, and Le (2018) of high school freshmen students found that despite gender stereotypes that say boys are more likely to be the problem students in school, the study revealed that girl students constitute the majority of youths struggling the most academically, socially, and behaviorally. Students were assessed using a questionnaire that asks them to rate the importance of social skills across seven domains: communication, cooperation, assertion, responsibility, empathy, engagement, and self-control. Interestingly, girls who placed little value on social skills actually earned lower grades, had more disciplinary referrals, and saw poorer attendance records than boys with similar responses. The researchers reported that while some prior studies suggested that changing students' ideas and engagement using social skills could improve academic performance, their study found that promoting social skills was likely to have only a small impact on boys' attendance and grades, whereas *greater improvements would more likely be seen in girls' grades, attendance and behaviors* (Tan et al., 2018, p. 1). Even this current research implies competency versus confidence appear as disparities. The concept that a girl's misbehavior is a flaw in her character and must be "worked on" while a boy's misbehavior is a desire to assert himself feeds into long-standing stereotypical behaviors into adulthood.

Without careful monitoring by school leaders, gender bias is often embedded and reinforced in textbooks, resources, curriculum, lessons, and the interactions with teachers. Therefore, culturally proficient educators must be prepared to assess, monitor, interrupt, and replace culturally destructive instructional practice with inclusive, intentional practices focused on equity, including gender equity.

## MORE ABOUT SHAPING YOUNG MINDSETS AND BEHAVIORS

Children are bombarded by descriptors of who they are through media and social media, fashion, and the toy–gaming industry as well as parenting. Their future identities are shaped by audio and visual depictions of a traditional binary world of males and females. However, superheroes are beginning to shift from predominately White males, like Superman, Capitan America, Iron Man, and Batman, to heroes of color and female heroes, such as Wonder Woman, Black Panther, and Captain Marvel. TV commercials include Gay parents, biracial couples, and blended families. Words used to describe fictitious characters or images guide young learners to see themselves and shape their future selves.

Table 3.1 presents a word bank of alternative visions for traditional selves. What might be additional words you would put on the lists?

Myra and David Sadker's observation made in 1994 resonates today: *Until educational sexism is eradicated, more than half of our children will be shortchanged and their gifts lost to society* (p. 3).

Given the impact and influence of traditional words and stories that remain part of today's vernacular, curriculum and supporting materials must be

**TABLE 3.1** Alternative, Inclusive Word Choices for All-Gender Children and Youth

| ALL-GENDERS: ALTERNATIVE/ADDITIONAL WORD CHOICES TO PRINCESS/ BEAUTIFUL AND PRINCE/HANDSOME | |
| --- | --- |
| Smart | Caring |
| Unique | Vibrant |
| Original | Witty |
| Inventive | Funny |
| Resourceful | Decisive |
| Imaginative | Focused |
| Brave | Creative |
| Thoughtful | Spirited |
| Strong | Insightful |
| **Other Word Choices?** | |
| | |

gender-fair, inclusive, accurate, affirmative, and representative of all students. Teachers who are aware of gender bias tendencies will use instructional strategies to combat bias in their classrooms. We see urgency in this instructional message. Being aware of the lack of gender balance as indicated through research of women as educational leaders, all educators must transfer this knowledge to our girls in the classrooms as we prepare them to be competent and confident future leaders, whether leading our schools or other organizations.

## TELL A DIFFERENT STORY

As women educational leaders, we have studied the barriers that many women face when seeking educational leadership positions, and we offer a counternarrative and appropriate strategies to confront and overcome these barriers. You may want to refer to Chapter 2 for a review of the Barriers to Cultural Proficiency. As noted in Chapter 2, the Tools of Cultural Proficiency form the foundation for assessing equity journeys and implementing action plans for shifting school district leaders' actions from inequitable practices to equitable practices. With this chapter, we present and illustrate in depth the first of the four Tools of Cultural Proficiency, Overcoming these Barriers.

The individual and institutional **barriers** that women face are categorized as follows:

- Being unaware of the school or district's need to adapt to having women leaders at all levels

- Denying the existence of sexism and gender inequities as systemic oppression

- Denying the existence of systemic privilege and entitlement that favors male leaders

- Resisting change that aids in attracting, recruiting, and mentoring women in leadership positions

These barriers are real and undeniable in today's educational context. We explored what some female leaders had to say about their own barriers.

### Gathering Narrative Data

Earlier in this book, we three coauthors described a small gathering of women—the Women in Education Leadership Retreat (WELR)—to help us identify the barriers that hindered their progress toward their career goals, as well as identify the support factors that assisted women leaders on their career journeys. We had hoped to gather 10 to 15 women on a Saturday morning for coffee and brunch to respond to our two questions. Much to our surprise and appreciation, almost 30 women joined us. Many of the women told us the invitation and the questions intrigued them because no one had ever asked them about barriers or support factors to their career goals. We found these women to be everyday women educational leaders doing their jobs well. We had planned an agenda that included an opening strategy called Go 'Round. We would simply "go around" the room, and each guest would respond to the following prompts:

> *No one had ever asked them about barriers or support factors to their career goals.*

*Who are you?*

*What do you do and where?*

*What inspired/intrigued you to be here today?*

We had allowed 25 minutes for this strategy, including time for the three of us to respond to the prompts. We could not stop the responses! An hour and a half later, each woman had spoken and had told amazing stories about why she was inspired to attend. They told stories of struggles, inspiration, heartbreak, and motivation. The women needed and wanted to tell their stories. Additionally, they wanted to hear each other's stories.

> *An hour and a half later, each woman had spoken and had told amazing stories about why she was inspired to attend. They told stories of struggles, inspiration, heartbreak, and motivation. The women needed and wanted to tell their stories. Additionally, they wanted to hear each other's stories.*

## TODAY'S CONTEXT AND BARRIERS

Linda Lambert and Mary Gardner (2009) described in their research numerous barriers that got in the way of women as educational leaders. Over a decade later, many of these barriers still exist:

- Isolation: Breaking the mold is lonely work.
- Multiple roles: Competing demands of family and work; long hours; perceived tension
- Absence of role models: Being quiet; fearing the show of emotions; wondering about unwritten and ambiguous dress codes
- Master narrative: Pleasing others and caring for others
- Male-dominated culture: Being harassed; being joked about; being quiet; being fired for no cause
- Continued absence of health and family care: Fearing women's health issues; fearing gender identity and sexual harassment.

Several of the interviewees' stories mentioned earlier revealed incidents that occurred 20 and 30 years ago; yet other women told similar experiences that had occurred within the past ten years, five years, and even one year ago. As many male leaders contend the glass ceiling has been shattered and the playing field has been leveled, women continue to find the contrary. In addition to the glass ceiling, the retreat participants identified key pitfalls to their progress, including marginalization, lack of mentoring and sponsorship, stereotyping, and discrimination. Cultures within the larger group of women were well represented at the WELR. Women of color and women of the LGBTQIA+ community clearly identified existing barriers that many White, heterosexual women do not encounter or see. Generational differences were made clearer in the stories the women shared. One participant said,

> If you're a Gay person (like me), you always have to come out to every single person you know. None of you, if you're straight, have to do that.

Historical societal constructs of gender and race became evident as women expressed their journeys navigating multiple cultural boundaries in addition to gender barriers. Women raising families and women choosing not to raise families spoke of expectations that served as barriers, irrespective of parenthood or not.

Numerous examples cited by the participants directly aligned to the Barriers identified in the Cultural Proficiency Framework (Chapter 2):

- System of Oppression
- System of Privilege and Entitlement
- Unawareness of the Need to Adapt
- Resistance to Change

The WELR participants recognized and acknowledged the barriers that we address and overcome.

## Systems of Oppression and Entitlement

The women leaders described themselves as not being positioned well to qualify for executive leadership positions as opposed to the entitled, traditional leadership roles occupied by their male counterparts. Many women reported following a "traditional female route," including the roles of elementary teacher, elementary principal, or curriculum and instruction–related pathways as opposed to athletic coach, high school principal, or district office administrator in human relations (or business or technology)—roles that serve as pathways to assistant superintendent and superintendent. Women, in contrast, served as department- or grade-level chairs, teachers on special assignment (TOSA), district curriculum or professional development coordinators, directors of curriculum, assistant superintendent of several districts, and finally, superintendent. In many ways, the various positions held by women on their leadership journeys affected the ways they were viewed as the "fit" for executive leadership positions (Wallace, 2014). Thus, the women leaders reported statements like these to be uttered by supervisors:

> It's not your time yet.

> You need more experience.

> You are not proficient with budgets and the political aspects of the job yet.

*This district isn't ready for a female assistant superintendent for personnel or business yet.*

*I can't promote you now—you are too important for the work of your department.*

*You are not strong enough.*

*This job would require you to have the keys to the total facility. You would be required to stay late and lock up. I just can't ask a woman to do that.*

As female leaders, may we be so bold as to suggest that women be given the keys both figuratively and literally!

## Unawareness of a Need to Adapt

This barrier—the Unawareness of a Need to Adapt—was filled with stories of lingering stereotypes, biases, and misinformation. Perceptions that women need to spend more time with family and that men have more time to work hard and get the job done have a lack of evidence. Women leaders shared experiences of having the tissue box moved toward them during difficult conversations or being stereotyped by the way they dressed, their accent, and even their tears. One retreat participant shared that her supervisor accused her of being "flirty" because of her accent. The informal, lighthearted, two-way conversation was clearly on his terms. Another participant shared her experience with her supervisor following a high-stakes, potentially volatile community meeting that she chaired. She had shared her passion for students through her tears. Her male supervisor cautioned her that she shouldn't show her emotions in public that way. She responded to him,

> *Do not mistake my tears for a sign of weakness. My ability to emote, feel, and be vulnerable and share my passion for our students is indeed my greatest strength.*

Women participants of the LGBTQIA+ community reported having to protect their identity to avoid professional and personal harm. Women leaders of color spoke of being frequently asked to give extra time and prove their qualifications. They also described their feelings of isolation accompanied by a sense of pride when they realized they were the "only woman of color" in the room. Women of color spoke of being targeted to serve and lead groups who looked like them, with an incorrect assumption that they were not qualified to lead organizations for all leaders in the organization. One female of color participant added,

> *As I looked around, I noticed we (WOC) were assigned to be in charge of equity plans, diversity recruitment for people of color, newcomer committees, newly formed diversity and equity departments, and all things diversity. But I was denied a principalship.*

*I am often baffled and appalled by the fact that I was not permitted to wear pants to school until I was in high school in the early 1970s in a public school district in Southern California.* —Retired White female principal

Attention to women's issues related to public education came by protest and mandate in the 20th century. Finally, with the passage of Title IX, the federal civil rights law of 1972, school districts were prohibited from discriminatory practices and programs based on gender. Typically, Title IX has applied to girls' and boys' athletic programs. Although this comprehensive federal law offered protection to girls and women, school districts today continue to grapple and wrestle with policies and practices to ensure that the law is followed and respected.

Within organizations at the district and site level, the inability to recognize the need to change is often reflected in members' daily policies and practices. As leaders deconstruct educational practices, we find that our practices are often inconsistent with the stated values of the organization and present themselves as barriers to success for women and girls. Such practices may serve as door closers rather than door openers for gender equity and access. (Arriaga & Lindsey, 2016). Culturally proficient leaders ensure the alignment of the stated values with the actions of the organization. *We value and treat all people equitably with dignity and respect* is a mission statement that is frequently found in the guiding principles of a district, yet the practices of gender equity may be misaligned with the stated goal and without fidelity to the intention of Title IX. The stated mission statement that follows can be questioned by the examination of the daily practices of the organization.

Our Mission: *We value and treat all people equitably with dignity and respect.*

- Do your coaches of male athletes earn more than your coaches of female athletes?

- Do you tolerate language that demeans and reinforces the socialization of girls being inferior, such as *cry like a girl, throw like a girl,* or *[be] weak like a girl*?

- Do you see gender disproportionality in data such as suspensions, extracurricular opportunities, technology courses, and athletics?

- Do your female athletes play on Thursday nights in the small gym and the male athletes play on Friday nights in the large gym?

- Do you omit or have a disproportionate number of women contributions in your curriculum?

- Are students taught gender stereotypes through your actions, such as boys' and girls' lines, different-colored robes based on gender for graduation, or dress codes specific to females?

- Do you consistently hire males in leadership positions at the high schools and executive-cabinet level to include roles such as superintendent, maintenance director, chief business official, and chief technology officer?

- Do you refer to the women in certain positions as *the girls* or *gals?*

- Do you consistently present the pronoun *he* in memos, board policies, and district documents?

- Do you have policies that negatively impact the female, such as no job shares or no breastfeeding accommodations?

- Are women of color in targeted roles, such as director of diversity, bilingual coordinator, principal of a high-poverty school, or newcomer coordinator?

If the answer is yes to any of these questions, do you have the will and the vision to open the doors that are closed to females in the organization (Arriaga & Lindsey, 2016)? More important than the sample questions and sample vision are the questions raised within the organization. What are your practices, policies, or values that are not aligned to the vision of your organization? What is the process to examine your practices for gender inequity? What is the process to address and change the practices? Is your organization ready to accept *that's the way we've always done it* as NOT the *way it should always be?*

## Resistance to Change

The glass ceiling effect was clearly identified as the Barrier of Resistance to Change. Districts are frequently identified as reluctant to hire women as superintendents, business leaders, technology specialists, and human resource leaders. This is especially true among women of color. Numerous executive women of color interviewees told one researcher (Tulshyan, 2015), *The glass ceiling metaphor doesn't work for us* (p. 1). She instead described it as a "concrete ceiling." Not only is the concrete ceiling reported to be more difficult to penetrate, but women of color say they cannot see through it to glimpse the corner office (Tulshyan, 2015). Our WELR participants shared with us these quotes after their interviews:

> We already have one female high school principal. Don't you think we are going too far if we appointed another female? —Comment from male mentor to female applicant

> You are the top candidate, but it's his turn. —Comment from older female mentor to female applicant

*The men on the committee would not look at me when I spoke or when they spoke. They only looked at each other. I was the first female superintendent. Finally, I said, "I'd like for you to look at me when you have something to say." After that, things changed for the better. —White female veteran superintendent*

## MENTORS ARE IMPORTANT ALLIES

Numerous retreat women reported the lack of female mentoring. Mentors were listed as Joe, Bob, Randy, José, Rich, and Jerry. The commonality among the attendees was that the majority of their mentoring came from men. We even noticed that sometimes women reported other women as barriers by being territorial with a "pull up the ladder—I'm already up" attitude. Traditionally, women have been competitive with each other due to the scarce number of women who actually make it to the top. Melinda Gates (2019) discovered in her journey to help women around the world that the best way for women to make progress is to work together. Here is a line from Gates's book that resonates for us:

*Our call is to lift women up—and when we come together in this cause, we are the lift.* (p. 4)

Women benefit from cultures of collaboration over competitive environments. Shelly Zalis (2019) confirms that women who belong to a circle of close female work contacts are more likely to land top-paying executive positions with greater authority than other females or males without those connections. The opportunity to share experiences of unconscious bias, discrimination, and the brunt of other stereotypical behavior builds and strengthens the inner circles of trust necessary to navigate the waters of gender inequities. The bonds formed by female mentors and sponsors provide meaningful connections, which result in a powerful force to propel women of confidence and competence. Women must find their tribe and join together in the journey.

> *The male mentor is positioned to gain information through the relationship by truly understanding the experiences of the female leader and thus becoming a gender inequity disruptor and an ally in the partnership.*

Concomitantly, we address our value of the male mentor and the mentor–mentee relationship specifically in Chapter 6. The relationship must be one of dual support with an avoidance of a heroic, rescue effort by the male. The male mentor is positioned to gain information through the relationship by truly understanding the experiences of the female leader and thus becoming a gender inequity disruptor and an ally in the partnership. When the relationship is not one of dual partnership, women participants stated that male mentors periodically contribute to the barriers by offering advice such as this:

> Don't apply for that. It's a male-dominated position. We need your expertise in the position you are currently holding.

> You're not ready yet. You need more experience and more education. You'll need your doctorate before you think of applying as assistant superintendent.

According to a female assistant principal, one of her male principals told her,

> If you want to become a principal in this district, you'll need to start acting more like a man.

Imagine her disappointment when her self-appointed mentor spoke those words to her.

## SUPPORTING WOMEN EDUCATIONAL LEADERS

Overcoming barriers to equitable educational practices requires a sense of moral purpose. The Guiding Principles of Cultural Proficiency foster the development of a set of core values focused on equity and inclusion. These values serve as a moral framework for conducting one's self, school, and district in an ethical manner. The Guiding Principles serve as guides for who we say we are as leaders. These core values are also the representation of the district for serving historically marginalized groups (Lindsey, Nuri-Robins, Terrell, & Lindsey, 2019). Clearly, the challenges the female participants at WELR overcame and the successes they experienced relied on their talents and expertise, as well as support and encouragement from mentors throughout their careers.

As a historically marginalized group, female educational leaders have unique cultural needs. Overcoming barriers to equity requires women leaders to push through the limitations that have been set upon and in front of them. Perseverance to overcome barriers sometimes emerges through external recognition and nudges, as heard in some comments expressed from many of the women leaders at WELR. Some participants spoke about nurturers who saw beyond what they thought of themselves; other mentors recognized the interviewees' capabilities and, through encouragement and support, helped set in motion the trajectory of their leadership careers. Leader after leader referred to the *taps on the shoulder* from their principals, HR directors, and professors. Nurturers seem to know that those invitations to serve on teacher-leader committees, strategic-planning teams, and organizational boards are the seeds that foster women leadership.

Female leaders also spoke of the support and motivation coming from members of the school communities in which they served. Through the development of deeper relationships with students and families, they were compelled to *do more,* form community partnerships, and extend their educational degrees for the specific purpose of building their capacity to better serve members of marginalized groups. One female administrator shared,

> [M]y life was changing, and my lens was changing by immersing myself in the communities that I was working in and getting to know those families in the way that I did and becoming really vulnerable myself.

Several women leaders shared that once they were set on the pathway of educational leader, support from members in professional organizations helped them sustain their careers.

## Gender Is Not Monocultural

In our quest to be culturally proficient, we understand that women as a group are not monocultural. As an example of the Guiding Principle *Diversity exists within group identity,* the diversity amongst women leaders is vast, significant, and referred to as intersectionality of identity. Women identify by their gender, sexual orientation, language, faith, ableness, and ethnicity. Intersectionality is the overlapping structures of subordination in which marginalized people are situated. This intersection of identities manifests itself in the consequences of interactive oppressions, the elimination of people's experiences at the intersections of multiple oppressions, and the cultural construction of identities that result in negative stereotypes that are used to further discredit marginalized experiences (Agosto & Roland, 2018). One educational leader who is female, Black, and Gay, shared that she is all of these identities, experiences, and perspectives. We explore *intersectionality* in greater depth in Chapter 5.

While WELR participants appreciated the camaraderie that existed in the all-female leadership cohort, one woman wanted everyone to understand that an important element of gatherings is this:

> The intentionality around forming the network and forming profound relationships also helps you professionally. . . . Strength comes not from my family only but my professional family. That's how I've met so many people.

When the Guiding Principles of Cultural Proficiency are used as the foundation for supporting the development of women in leadership, the individual, organization, and community benefit and thrive.

## FEMALE AND MALE LEADERS: DO GENDER DIFFERENCES MAKE A DIFFERENCE?

No longer do researchers ask, *Can women lead?* Today, given successful women leaders in the business world—especially at the corporate level, politics, and education—that question has been resolved. Over the past decade, women leaders have achieved high-level positions in countries throughout the world and continue to reach CEO positions in many corporations, as well as becoming high-ranking officers in the military (Hoyt et al., 2010). So a question for current researchers is this: *Who are better leaders: women or men?* Based on Eagly and her colleagues' meta-analyses (2003, 2007), a focus of inquiry is actual leadership behaviors. Since traditionally—and currently in education leadership—men hold more leadership positions, it makes sense that men's traits and behaviors are typically viewed as the standards for *the successful leader*. In other words, if more men are in leadership roles than women, then assumptions lead some people to believe that men are more successful leaders than women. Assumptions then become stereotypes that become expectations for performance evaluations that become barriers for female leaders' career advancement.

Historically, women may not have *fit the mold* of leaders in many fields (military, political and public institutions, and science fields). However, those assumptions/stereotypes and expectations/performance/barriers do not hold in today's complex work worlds (Stempel, Rigotti, & Mohr, 2015). For example, women have proven themselves highly skillful and successful as astronauts, military officers, political candidates, and superintendents of large school districts. Some researchers (Eagly, 2007; Eagly et al., 2003; Eagly & Karau, 2002) studied female and male leadership roles and identified particular leadership styles based on gender differences. Men seem to be viewed as *transactional managers* (hold clear expectations, provide appropriate rewards and consequences for employees' behaviors, act as agent or representative for employees, and observe for errors to correct through action and inspiration). However, women leaders tend to be viewed as *transformational leaders* (actively displaying supportive, inclusive, visionary, collaborative/communal, and appreciative behaviors), which aligns well with female-specific traits (Eagly et al., 2003; Eagly & Karau, 2002).

Once styles and traits were assigned as gender-specific, male or female, to the leaders' actual behaviors, then assumptions and stereotypes were often used for recruiting, hiring, and retaining leaders. Generally speaking, women's traits did not match the dominant role of *male as agent and manager*; therefore, women leaders (as described by work and social traits) had to be both agent/manager and collaborative/communal in their behaviors. These notions of female–male leadership traits, behaviors, and styles have persisted throughout the early 21st century. If the male agent/manager (transactional style) is viewed as the standard, typical successful leader, then a female collaborative/communal leader (transformational style) will have to make adjustments toward becoming more agent/manager-like—that is, more like a man. However, if both styles are viewed and valued as necessary and successful, then incongruence between the gender-specific roles might diminish (Stempel et al., 2015). Once a more transformational leadership style is viewed as more successful and typical, women leaders might be more highly valued and sought after.

Interestingly, researchers indicate that even when women display the exact same behaviors as their male counterparts (agent/manager), they are still viewed as less appreciated or seen as less-than-successful (i.e., deficit-oriented) leaders. Numerous researchers (Eagly, 2007; Stempel et al., 2015) concur that traits and styles described as female-specific leadership behaviors may serve as an advantage for career development and concomitantly be viewed as a stereotypical disadvantage. These perceptions and actions reinforce barriers to promotions and retention of female leaders by male-dominated boards, HR perceptions by male and female leaders (men as managers), and male mentors (act more like a man). Collectively, as culturally proficient educators we must work to remove these long-standing, now-outdated perceptions. More inclusive actions are embedded in responses to our question, *In what ways might educational leaders make decisions and take intentional actions toward creating and sustaining a gender-neutral and/or equitable environment in our schools and districts?*

Culturally proficient practices allow for assets-based actions to overcome barriers imposed by persistent stereotypes, long-held perceptions, and inequitable hiring practices against nondominant, marginalized groups. Together, we can work against these persistent inequities and ensure equitable attention be brought to hiring practices, mentorship development, and leadership development.

## FROM GENDER INEQUITY TO GENDER EQUITY

Unlike the research of the late 20th century that emphasized the numerical representation of women in leadership roles, our narrative data focuses on the everyday female leader and the relationships of social/cultural interactions of gender and power in women's career journeys. A cultural, sociological view treats leadership and leaders as a conceptual lens through which to view the nature, purpose, and capacities of educational systems and organizations to reform and indeed rethink about their practices in more socially just ways. These narratives add to today's conversations about how women leaders want to be identified and how that identity should not serve as a barrier for career advancement (Blackmore, 2013). Culturally proficient leaders can provide substantive and normative alternatives to how we theorize and practice leadership.

### Confronting and Removing the Barriers

The identified barriers of gender equity cannot be summed up in a checklist for completion, but many strategies and procedures will assist all people within the organization to engage in rich dialogue through the examination and deconstruction of current practices. Referring to the four areas of barriers—system of oppression, systemic effects of privilege and entitlement, unawareness of the need to adapt, and resistance to change—the following actions are offered as places to begin on the journey of gender equity, access, and renewed opportunity.

- Start early and recognize that our girls are programmed to become women. Eliminate and disrupt use of materials, policies, practices, procedures, and professional development that promote gender inequities in our classrooms.

- Promote women in roles that are pathways to executive leadership positions as they begin their careers.

- Provide networks of mentoring to include training for the mentors specific to the female protégée and leader.

- Implement networks of mentoring for women by women.

- Ensure that the unique needs of women of color are deeply embedded into all recruitment and retention efforts.

- Provide professional development for men and women in leadership to recognize and remove the barriers that are in place at the site and district level.

- Examine all practices, policies, and procedures with the lens of cultural proficiency toward gender equity.

- Recognize and respond to the stereotypical practices of positioning women of color in designated roles.

- Recognize and respond to the marginalization of our colleagues in the LGBTQIA+ community.

- Be conscious and responsive to stereotypes and negative perceptions of women in the workplace.

- Examine the interview process to ensure it is not a process of embedded, unconscious gender bias.

- Assess the stated values of the organization and the actual actions that exist. Do your leadership actions reflect the district's stated values?

## Our Time Is Now!

> *Be that woman who fixes another woman's crown without telling the world that it was crooked.* —Anonymous

We shared these extraordinary stories of sincere, well-prepared, everyday women educational leaders to provide a frame for working toward gender equity. Women leaders will no longer be seen as the extraordinary candidate to meet unrealistic expectations placed on them by systems of oppression and entitlement. Women leaders with their male and female mentors will tell their stories of leadership actions focused on socially just schools and communities.

As millions of women march around the globe, carrying signs of "Nevertheless, she persisted," the feminist battle cry is louder and clearer than ever before. The #MeToo and Time's Up movements have given rise to a platform for all voices to be heard with the urgency of a new day. A day is near when injustices and inequities will not be tolerated and women will not be silenced. The historic number of women who ran for office and won in 2018 was not just the crack in the glass ceiling but a powerful wave that is sweeping the nation. May the momentum continue to rise as the *Wonder Woman* movie quickly rose to become one of the highest-grossing super hero movies and a Hijab-wearing Barbie became available for children. Every woman, man, and child is invited to join the movement of the removal of barriers and the stand for *empow(her)ment* of every individual. Yes, it *is* about time. Yes, it is *our* time to stand, march, sit in, speak up, and persist against all barriers to gender equity.

## Looking Through the Window

As you look through the windows of your organization, what are some identifiable barriers to gender equity that do not reflect the stated values of the organization? What steps can be taken to disrupt the gender-biased actions that lead to barriers for women i leadership? In what ways might you and your colleagues identify gender inequities in you organization?

_____

_____

_____

_____

_____

# CHAPTER 4

# Moving Forward With Guiding Principles

*Each time a woman stands up for herself, without knowing it possibly, without claiming it, she stands up for all women.*

—Maya Angelou

 **LOOKING in the MIRROR**

Look in your mirror: As you examine your own reflection, think about what deeply held values and beliefs guide your decisions and actions as a leader. Now, make a list of your top ten values. What's on your list? Often, leaders list words like *ethics, integrity, family, honesty,* and *fairness.* Look at your list again. What best describes the essence of you—that if something was taken off your list, you would no longer be you? Now, mark five items off your list. What are your top five values? Top three? As you read this chapter about Guiding Principles for Cultural Proficiency, think about the core values that help determine who you are as a leader. Have you ever been asked to leave part of who you are outside the school site or district?

_____

_____

_____

_____

_____

## THE IMPACT OF SUPPORT

Overcoming the barriers toward equitable educational practices requires a sense of moral purpose. The Guiding Principles of Cultural Proficiency foster the development of a set of core values focused on equity and inclusion. These values serve as a moral framework for conducting one's self in an ethical manner and fostering school and district policies and practices that do the same. The Guiding Principles serve to support ourselves and inform others as to who we say we are as a system. Strong values are easily articulated as expressions of the culture of businesses, organizations, and certainly school districts. However, incorporating those values throughout the systems and structures of schools and districts is much more difficult. Ever harder are the behaviors of a leader to hold people in the organization accountable for policies, practices, and procedures that are consistent with the vision, mission, and the values of the organization. If a school site or district leader can do this, then she or he has learned not only the importance of a strong core culture, but also how to create an environment in which all members of the community understand their roles in maintaining that strong, positive culture. Vision statements convey espoused values; policies and practices reveal who you are by what you say and what you do. Do our actions reflect our values, and do our values reflect our actions (Arriaga & Lindsey, 2016)?

A tool that will help leaders close this gap and answer the question *Are we who we say we are?* is the Guiding Principles of Cultural Proficiency (Lindsey, Nuri-Robins, Terrell, & Lindsey, 2019). The Guiding Principles follow:

- Culture is a predominant force.
- People are served in varying degrees by the dominant culture.
- People have individual and group identities.
- Diversity within cultures is vast and significant.
- Each cultural group has unique cultural needs.
- The best of both worlds enhances the capacity of all.
- The family, as defined by each culture, is the primary system of support in the education of children.
- School systems must recognize that marginalized populations have to be at least bicultural and that this status creates a distinct set of issues to which the system must be equipped to respond.
- Inherent in cross-cultural interactions are dynamics that must be acknowledged, adjusted to, and accepted. (Lindsey et al., 2019, p. 82)

These core values are also representative of a district that is successful in serving historically marginalized groups and are commonly applied to monitor both individual and organizational actions in support of removing barriers to female executive leaders (Lindsey et al., 2019).

## Actionable Ways to Apply the Guiding Principles in the Hiring Context

- Understanding that people (women) are served in varying degrees by the dominant culture requires leaders with power and influence over hiring decisions to seek out the voice of women in their organization to find out if the true culture and climate is congruent with the espoused culture and climate.

- Diversity within cultures is vast and different. Organizations seeking to eliminate gaps have abandoned the idea of hiring "quotas." Instead, leaders seeking to establish authentic equitable organizations continuously ask themselves these questions:

  - Who are the women leaders in my organization?

  - Is there predictability in the positions they hold?

  - In what ways have their strengths helped our system thrive?

  - In what ways might I use this information as a tool to sponsor them toward positions with greater oversight, influence, and impact?

Dynamics that must be acknowledged, adjusted to, and accepted are inherent in cross-cultural interactions. Clearly, the challenges the female participants at the Women in Education Leadership Retreat (WELR) overcame and the successes they experienced relied on their talents and expertise, as well as support and encouragement from mentors throughout their careers. From our research, three distinct themes surfaced as critical elements that support the development and advancement of women educational leaders: coaching, professional networks, and familial advocacy.

However, some aspiring female leaders can feel at times as though they are invisible, as they may receive limited or no encouragement, support, or sponsorship. Words have power, and the women leaders at WELR expressed the impact of the words that ushered them into greater levels of leadership. Mentor leaders who speak words of support for the leadership prowess and advancement of females seeking to have a greater system impact actually have much greater influence than they may realize as mentors. Words that may have seemed slightly important to mentors were life changing for WELR participants. Here are stories from three WELR participants:

> *Words have power, and the women leaders at WELR expressed the impact of the words that ushered them into greater levels of leadership.*

- *To get into my doctorate program, I needed a letter of recommendation. So I asked the superintendent at the time . . . [and] he put that I will be a fine superintendent one day. Well, that wasn't my goal. I was a coordinator at the time. But that has struck me and like you, I've kept that letter this whole [time]. I keep going back because I'm like, Wow, how did he know that?*

- *I had a principal who told me in my second year of teaching that I was going to be a principal. And she showed me how to navigate the system. And she helped me navigate that network, and the same thing happened when I became a principal. I had a strong female administrator, an assistant superintendent who helped me along the way.*

- *I have worked to establish a group of LGBT administrators because we are completely invisible. I want to create a future where we don't have to come out in our interviews, where we don't have to hide in our workplaces.*

Never discount any interactions among aspiring female leaders. In a society where sexism continues to play a significant role in the educational leadership pipeline, mentors—regardless of gender—must be intentional and take advantage of the opportunities to develop others with their words.

## The Potential and Power of Networking

Throughout our dialogue and discussion during the retreat, the spirit of collectivism clearly was a key ingredient in the support and success of WELR participants and served as a strong tool for their women leadership development. A collectivist holds the belief that systems (human and organizational) are better when the perspectives of all are considered and included—better in decision-making, better in serving marginalized students and families, better at supporting peers, and better at working to boost one another as female educational leaders. The idea of collectivism presented itself in the form of participants sharing about the stamina they draw from their partnerships in professional networks, community relationships, and familial support.

We also found in our conversations with many women leaders that professional support took the form of affinity groups that helped address specific identity and cultural needs. Spending time together allowed them to share their stories and find support. They enjoy attending conferences for women and specifically women of color.

Connection and partnerships have always been powerful tools to overcome exclusion and isolation. A goal of all educational organizations must be to encourage and support active participation of rising women leaders.

## Bravery + Vulnerability = Courage

How brave are you when it comes to taking risks? Dr. Brené Brown (2017), grounded-theory expert, says that *our ability to be daring leaders will never be greater than our capacity for vulnerability* (p. 11). Leading to ensure all students experience school in an equitable and just manner is a cornerstone of culturally proficient practices, which require leaders to rely on visceral courage (Kugler & Stanley, 2012). Educational scholars such as Theoharis (2007) have long asserted that courage is a necessary criterion in leading for social justice. Employing courageous leadership practices can have a different impact depending on the sex/gender of the educational leader. Culture is a predominant force that shapes how we interpret information we take in. What may be seen as innovative and creative leadership methods for males is frequently frowned upon and questioned for female leaders. Rather than being seen as courageous trailblazers, female leaders may be seen as moving the system too quickly or lacking in their understanding of effective change management practices (Martin, 2011). As a result, women leaders are often concerned that they will be held to greater and unrealistic expectations for school harmony and perfected leadership practices. WELR participants shared their insights of the importance of networking with mentors (both women and men) who helped them navigate complex change and critical decisions in a way that was courageous, strategic, and led to more effective and socially just outcomes for their underserved students and staff. The dialogue among WELR participants emphasized the courage needed to move forward:

> *Courageous leadership and specific strategies aren't mutually exclusive. Professional and moral support play significant roles toward preparing women leaders for middle and upper levels of district leadership and retaining them in the field.*

- *One thing that I would say is all of the folks who've mentored me, male and female, have helped me be courageous. They've helped me make decisions that were outside of the box. And they helped me with the strategies to do that.*

- *What supported me is other women showing me how to be courageous in a strategic way to get what I needed for my students.*

- *So I just never would have that conversation—it was simple . . . but just having somebody say do it, you can do it, and here's how to do it . . . I appreciate that.*

Courageous leadership and specific strategies aren't mutually exclusive. Professional and moral support play significant roles toward preparing women leaders for middle and upper levels of district leadership and retaining them in the field. Strong core values for equity and access for all students help determine behaviors aligned with those values.

## Familial Support

Women leaders often have a foot in both worlds of school leadership and home management. Unlike many male education leaders, women who are parents and lead schools, departments, and districts also take a primary role in childrearing. These women must be bicultural and navigate two worlds; they must

- maintain and manage a supportive home environment; and
- lead with integrity in the work environment.

Navigating in and through these two cultural environments, women leaders deal with the constraints and unreasonable beliefs, values, and assumptions held about them in each of these worlds. The experiences held by WELR participants were no exception, and their reflections on the effect of family (immediate and extended) support were prevalent. The role that spousal/partner support plays is critical toward a woman's career flourishing. Recent literature from Hideg and Shen (2019) indicates that *the role of career support from intimate partners may have a significant impact on advancing into executive leadership roles* (p. 290). Without the support, committed relationships and marriages floundered and/or ended, yet others thrived when the support was present.

- *So one thing I was thinking about is the conversations that we have as women, as spouses, and the support that your spouse can either have or not have for you in your career. I talked to a teacher, and she said her husband was a principal. And she says, "I would like to be a principal too, but if I am not there for my kids, who will be there? It's only me." And I think that as we go forward as educational leaders, we [women leaders] do forget that our spouses are there to help us; men never forget that.*

- *You know, I had one spouse that didn't support me, and . . . now I have a new spouse who does support me. And I think that is a really, really important thing.*

- *And then being a mother of a son who talks about, you know, "Mom, I'm really proud of you being that strong person" and has forgiven me—or at least allowed me to forgive myself—for the long hours, the not being there. I think back to the conversations when he was in the first grade and we went to a birthday party one Saturday—when the stay-at-home moms said to me, "Wow, you're Sam's mom? I didn't even know he had a mom."*

The Cultural Proficiency Framework helps us understand that marginalized leaders—women leaders—thrive when the best of both worlds are harnessed. WELR participants expressed how their personal experiences served to shape their worldview and how those experiences fostered support, access, and inclusion for the working mothers of their students.

- *So once I became the principal and I [talked] to the moms who [had] the opportunity, I challenged them. I said, "Reach out to the working moms because, guys, guess what, I'm . . . that's me." I said, "There are moms at my son's school who are doing things I can't do, but I also want to be called in," so remind each other of that.*

WELR participants used this same critical worldview to serve as advocates to ensure that rising women leaders (formal and informal) have the support they need to thrive in their work settings.

- *I had a leader as I was an up-and-coming teacher, and she courageously fought for me. I mean, she had to go to a director and say, "This is an FMLA issue." So I have to be willing to go against what was status quo, too.*

When the Guiding Principles of Cultural Proficiency are used as the foundation for supporting the development of women in leadership, then the individual, organization, and community can benefit and thrive. In the face of being pulled in multiple directions, questioned about leadership abilities and decisions, and remaining focused for the purpose of ensuring that underserved students learn in environments of equity and inclusion, women in educational leadership must remember that they are "more than enough." These are the words that the 96-year-old mother of one of the WELR leaders shared with her: *You are more than enough.*

## Looking Through the Window

As you examine the district where you work, check the alignment of espoused values and values-in-use. The espoused values are published as vision and mission statements and answer the question *Who are we?* The organization's values-in-use are revealed as actual actions and evidenced by decisions made about policies, practices, procedures related to resource allocation, hiring practices, and academic procedures. Values-in-use answer the question *Are we who we say we are?* In what ways do the published values of your organization align with their actions?

_____

_____

_____

_____

_____

# CHAPTER 5

# Understanding Feminism, Identity, and Intersectionality

## Who Am I?

## Who Are We?

*A basic definition of feminism is that it is a movement to end sexism and sexist exploitation and oppression.*

—bell hooks (2000, p. 108)

 **LOOKING in the MIRROR**

Open a new, blank page on your computer. Or use a blank piece of paper. Write the following ten questions and answer each one before going to the next one.

1. Who am I?

2. Who am I?

3. Who am I?

4. Who am I?

5. Who am I?

6. Who am I?

7. Who am I?

*(Continued)*

(Continued)

8. Who am I?

9. Who am I?

And finally . . .

10. Who am I?

As you responded to each of the ten questions, what are some reactions you noticed abou yourself? What might be the purpose of this learning strategy? What might be some responses if you asked this question of members of your organization, school, or district: *Who are we?*

What are your thoughts about feminism, sexism, and intersectionality in relation to who yo are in the workplace?

_____

_____

_____

_____

_____

We wrote about the importance of knowing self and knowing the organization in earlier chapters. We also wrote extensively about self-imposed and systemic barriers that female leaders must recognize and overcome along their career paths. The purpose of this chapter is to expand on these concepts (the inside-out process and barriers) and illustrate why three terms—*feminism*, *sexism*, and *intersectionality*—are critical to understanding and overcoming systemic, intentional, entrenched, and inequitable barriers for female leaders.

First, we introduce numerous feminist theories to lay a foundation for knowing about forces that are already in place to counteract inequities for female leaders. Table 5.1 displays a summary of theories and descriptions of key concepts for each theory. You may recognize a description of why you have taken or plan to take a path toward gender equity. For generations, *feminism* has served as the pioneering launch point for confronting the many oppressions women experience. This chapter offers *feminism* as an overarching theoretical approach to help understand gender inequities, specifically.

Second, we offer an exploration of "intersectionality" as another way for *assessing cultural knowledge* and taking action toward equity. We give attention to the past research and current actions being taken; and we advocate for the importance of acknowledging identity and the multiple worlds in which women live; yet women are often perceived as monolithic. The nonbinary nature of gender and identity as described in today's social and educational contexts sheds light on the challenging, positive, and rewarding work of equity yet to be done. *Intersectionality* explores and expands our ways of understanding and confronting inequities identified as racism, sexism, and classism. As you read the following sections, keep this question in mind for further exploration: *What opportunities for supporting gender equity might this information about feminism and intersectionality provide me?*

## FEMINIST THEORIES CHALLENGE STATUS QUO SYSTEMS OF OPPRESSION

Feminism is both a scholarly area of study and a voice for change. Feminism, as we describe it here, is about using a lens to examine inequities of gender, race, and class within ourselves and our schools and districts (Lay & Daley, 2007). Using the lens of Cultural Proficiency allows us to view feminism with attention to difference, power, and social justice. No single feminism theory has yet evolved; however, concepts held in common across the theories include the following:

- Valuing women of color and all women

- Valuing each woman's experience

- Identifying oppressive conditions toward women

- Acknowledging women as gender-fluid and men and women as nonbinary

- Recognizing that factors, in addition to gender, impact and influence women's views and actions

Feminist researchers continue to study contexts, conditions, and concepts that will lead to developing strategies and actions for eliminating all forms of oppression and -isms. In our Introduction, we listed terms and definitions as they are used in this book, including *feminism theory*, *hostile sexism*, and *benevolent sexis*m. Our intent here is not to deliver fully developed scholarly descriptions of sexism and feminism; however, we offer a brief summary of the diversity and similarities among the theories for the purpose of knowing the foundations of work focused on gender equity. Table 5.1 reviews representative feminist theories from prominent researchers and related concepts. Please note that this list will grow and expand and deepen as society becomes increasingly attuned to issues of equity and access. It lists the theories, acknowledges researchers, and describes key concepts of each theory.

**TABLE 5.1** Feminist Theories, Researchers, and Concepts

| THEORY | REFERENCE | CONCEPTS |
|---|---|---|
| Individual transformation feminism | Collins, 1991 | Historical structures remain in place as institutions of male domination. Individuals may overcome barriers, but not enough to break patterns. |
| Black feminism | Collins, 1991, 2000 Crenshaw, 1989 Johnson, 1983 Kanneh, 1998 | Interlocking systems of oppression are based on race, gender, and class. Counter oppression is manifest through consciousness and empowerment. |
| Radical feminism | Ferguson, 1996 | Men's oppression and domination are natural phenomena and must be interrupted. |
| Lesbian feminism | Andermahr, Lovell, & Wolkowitz, 1997 Rich, 1986 | Since men dominate all women, lesbians established themselves as a distinct group to challenge male oppression at large. |
| Liberal feminism | Saulnier, 1996 | Women cannot be denied rights to receive education, vote, hold citizenship, make health choices, and develop financial independence. |
| Marxist feminism and material feminism | Donovan, 1993 MacKinnon, 1997 | Women emancipated themselves to the work world, providing them a pathway to capitalism and determining social and family values. Feminists advocated for pay for domestic labor. |
| Socialist feminism | Evans, 1995 | Activists demand all forms of oppression be eliminated. Women are advocates for differences irrespective of the context or group. |
| Postmodern feminism | Evans, 1995; Matthews, 2017 | Women struggle to see gender's relationship to a system of oppression; yet they see the equality of all genders, race, and sexuality as a way of reinforcing society roles. Value is placed on having achieved equality; therefore, there is no need for feminist actions. |

SOURCE: A summary of theories adapted from *A Critique of Feminist Theory*. Kay, Kathy, and Daley, James G. 2017, May, retrieved from doi:10.18060/131 August 21, 2019.

Table 5.1 traces feminist theory as the lived experiences of women in relationship to male domination and systemic oppression. Theoretical perspectives provide assumptions to guide questions in the quest to understand lived experiences. Challenging structures of domination and oppression using culturally proficient practices will lead to heightened levels of consciousness and actions focused on equitable access to participation in education, government, health choices, and financial independence. Disparities that flow from systemic oppression such as gender, sexuality, race, and social class come together when addressing the lived experiences of educators in our preK–12 schools.

### Reflection

Now that you've reviewed *feminism* as described in Table 5.1, in what ways might theory shape your thinking about actions needed for systemic changes focused on gender equity?

_____

_____

_____

_____

_____

## UNDERSTANDING INTERSECTIONALITY

The evolution of understanding that humans hold many characteristics that define the essence of who they are and how they navigate the world has led to the frequent use of "identity" nomenclature. For generations, the binary identity of male and female, posited by Geertz in 1973, was held as the standard for gender identity. In her 2016 article, Marecek outlines the 1979 work of researcher Rhoda Unger in which acceptance of this individualist frame of reference of gender as property to be held solely by males and females emerged in feminist literature. However, in recent years this popular individualist theory has been challenged (Marecek, 2016, p. 179). In 1989, Black feminist Kimberlé Crenshaw proposed a different theory regarding gender—one that suggested that, rather than seeing gender as the property of females and males (individualist internal frame of reference), seeing that gender is deeply intertwined in an external structuralist frame that includes race/ethnicity, class, and sex/gender (Agosto & Roland, 2018; Marecek, 2016). This external structure forms social constructs that lead to a systematized hierarchy of inequitable experiences undergirded by barriers such as a resistance to change, privilege, entitlement, and an unwillingness to adapt and oppression (Lindsey et al., 2019; Marecek, 2016). These barriers have led to inequitable experiences and have had a disproportionate impact on women of color (Crenshaw, 1989). Table 5.2 presents a comparison of the two theories.

To reiterate, we understand that women as a group are not monocultural. Consistent with one of the Guiding Principles of Cultural Proficiency (*Diversity exists within group identity*), the diversity among women leaders is vast,

**TABLE 5.2** Frames of Reference for Gender and Intersectionality

| INDIVIDUALIST MODEL | STRUCTURALIST MODEL |
| --- | --- |
| Clifford Geertz, 1973 | Kimberlé Crenshaw, 1989 |
| Conventional model of human existence | Intersectionality |
| Internal frame | External structuralist frame |
| Binary gender: Male and female | Hierarchy of social constructs of race/ethnicity, class, and sex/gender |
| Bounded and autonomous free agents | "Crossroads" of "multiple oppressions" |

significant, and can be referred to as the intersectionality of identity. As stated in Chapter 3, women may hold several identities. Yet intersectionality theory moves us beyond the general look at how women identify and compels us to look at how intersectionality serves to impede the attainment and success of women of color and all women in executive leadership roles due to intersectionality of race and gender as well as aspects of language, social class, and faith. For instance, we remind our readers that a singular focus on one identity—women—is often viewed as White women and takes away from solving the broader systemic problem. Diversity, equity, and inclusion work is about paying attention to the experiences of marginalized groups in order to correct collective biases and obstacles to ensure an equitable working environment. So our efforts must be focused on understanding the structuralist concept of intersectionality and lifting all who have been marginalized and minimized as a result (Agosto & Roland, 2018, Kim, 2008).

One WELR participant and educational leader who is female, Black, and Gay shared that she is all of these identities, experiences, and perspectives and with them come multiple oppressions. Intersectionality is the overlapping structures of subordination in which marginalized people are situated.

> *Yet intersectionality theory moves us beyond the general look at how women identify and compels us to look at how intersectionality serves to impede the attainment and success of women of color and all women in executive leadership roles due to intersectionality of race and gender as well as aspects of language, social class, and faith.*

Intersectionality manifests itself in the consequences of interactive oppressions, the elimination of people's experiences at the intersections of multiple oppressions, and the cultural construction of identities that result in negative stereotypes that are used to further discredit marginalized experiences (Agosto & Roland, 2018; Marecek, 2016). Intersectionality is often recognized in the research as two identity components, such as race and gender, but rarely does the research address multiple aspects of intersectionality. Too often, those on the outside who are *looking in* believe that the intersectionality of these many identities shape women in some cascading fashion—first female, then Latina, then mother—that forms a social justice view of female leadership. Instead, with deeper knowledge those in power come to understand that the many identities held by women are woven

> *Diversity, equity, and inclusion work is about paying attention to the experiences of marginalized groups in order to correct collective biases and obstacles to ensure an equitable working environment.*

together to create a unique and stronger alternative narrative and seek to elevate the narratives instead of marginalize (Agosto & Roland, 2018).

Women of color leading in the field of education are often impacted by multiple forces, buried under the experiences of White men, men of color, or White women (Crenshaw, 2016). With the vast access to White female teachers in the field of education, one would assume that school districts and boards are expressly positioned to increase the number of White women who are leading as a chief executive officer (CEO), chief information officer (CIO), or chief finance officer (CFO)—often referred to as the *c-suite*. The complexity of increasing the number of women of color is compounded by stereotypes, many driven by decades of media socialization. Black women are often depicted as caregivers, weak, or too gregarious, while Asian women are represented as meek and compliant. Latinas navigate a space sometimes between being perceived as "too White" by the Hispanic community and "too ethnic" by colleagues in the workplace. They grapple with the cultural stereotypical norms of passivity, submissiveness, and the perception they are better suited for nonscholarly work roles (Jackson et al., 2013). These views, coupled with generalized beliefs and values about women's domestic roles, place a myriad of barriers for women of color to climb the proverbial career ladder. This *labyrinth* (Sanchez-Hucles & Davis, 2010), what seems like an unending and winding path toward executive leadership, often requires negotiating unknown situations without the guidance of mentors in the field. Women of color are often left alone to find their way through the tumult of hidden norms and being held to different standards and expectations. These differing expectations are manifested through the questioning of wardrobe and hairstyle choices, as well as linguistic and verbal communication patterns. One WELR participant shared her dismay when she was questioned by her board of trustees regarding the absence of her wedding ring. She refrained from showing her dismay and responded that working seven days a week did not allow her to get to the jeweler and replace the missing stone.

## UNDERSTANDING THE IMPACT: MICRO- AND/OR MACROAGGRESSIONS

We discovered the hierarchy of identities impacted women at WELR in differing ways. Participants shared their experience navigating a whole host of microaggressions and how that requires leadership stamina that many male leaders don't experience and need not understand. One female principal of color shared,

> I'm constantly navigating who I am based on my gender and my race. I feel that both are often seen as barriers to overcome rather than assets and strengths.

More often than not, those who experience the oppressions of intersectionality are left with complicated reflections. For instance, one female wondered if she was not acknowledged at a networking event because she is female or because she is Latina. Some females are left to wonder if they weren't invited to participate in a leadership panel due to their accent related to their linguistic heritage or due to their gender. Regardless of the experience, the tenacity and resilience that these intimidating and oppressive experiences develop were prevalent amongst all retreat participants. Women leaders spoke of how their intersecting identities positively impacted their interactions with members of the communities in which they lead. As an Asian American female superintendent participant put it,

> A year ago when I became the superintendent, I was at back-to-school night and I saw one of my young Asian kids come up, and she was talking to her mom and she kept pointing to me. And then her mom walked over; we shook hands and she asked, "Are you really the person in charge here?" I said, No, I have five bosses, and they're in charge. But, yes, I lead this district.

The women leaders held a sense of pride for how their presence sent a statement of possibility to all students and families and particularly stakeholders from marginalized communities. For example, a female African American superintendent said,

> You know, when I began thinking about leaving education a couple of times, I was always inspired by someone that looks like me, the little girls or little boys. I've been the first in many places [cabinet, assistant superintendent] who is an African American female. When you see little girls that give you the look of awe, the look of "I want to be like you when I grow up"—when I have that thought about leaving, it's like I can't. I need to be here. So I'm inspired to be here to work to remove those barriers that are in the way of gender equity and for African American women.

Cindy Pace of the *Harvard Business Review* (2018) asserts that women of color have unique cultural needs in leadership development. Organizations must clearly understand the *emotional* tax paid on a daily basis when women of color feel they have to be quiet and reserved due to concerns about racial and gender bias—simply put, the organization is losing out on the many gifts and talents that women of color have to offer. Moreover, when assets aren't cultivated within this human resource group, there is a significant loss due to high levels of turnover (Travis, Thorpe-Moscon, & McCluney, 2018). As we said earlier, our focus for this book was not solely to call attention to the disparities and gender inequities between male and female school and district leaders. Those disparities lead to an additional focus for us. We want to call attention to the loss of learning and leading that occurs when women leaders are not present. We are better together. Students benefit when female and male leaders bring their best thinking and leading skills to schools.

## Digging Deeper Into Educational Leadership

A Guiding Principle of Cultural Proficiency asserts that people—in this case, women leaders of color—are served in varying degrees by the dominant culture. The dominant culture of school administration has left out the true voice of female leaders of color, including indigenous women, for too long. Their voices and expertise are often sought solely with respect to struggles of race relations in schools and students' learning disparities. Often, women of color and indigenous women are consulted or needed when complex decisions related to social issues such as boundary or demographic changes are discussed (Sanchez-Hucles & Davis, 2010). In most cases, the "input" sought is in the form of members of the dominant culture seeking to use the voice of women leaders of color to cosign decisions that have already been made. Furthermore, the adversarial and political natures of these topics has led to leaders who are women of color being reprimanded, reassigned, or even dismissed (Sanchez-Hucles & Davis, 2010).

While these school district areas are important and female leaders of color have background knowledge about these topics, they are not the only areas of expertise they have to offer. Women of color and indigenous women bring unique perspectives related to business operations and human resources. Analysts such as Monica Eaton-Cardone (2018) recognize that organizations with greater percentages of multicultural female leaders have an increase in net margins. In education, this equates to increased community business partnerships, innovative planning, attracting diverse talent, and successful grant procurement. These are just the tip of the iceberg for the benefits that multicultural female leadership affords. A concerted effort to foster equity, access, and inclusion for indigenous women and female leaders of color in educational leadership requires systemwide change efforts in educational organizations:

- Assess the espoused values of the organization and the actual actions that exist. Do your actions reflect your values? (Arriaga & Lindsey, 2016)

- Revise hiring practices to mitigate disproportionality in administrative assignments.

- Intentionally develop mentorship *and* sponsorship programming that takes into consideration the unique needs of women of color and indigenous women leadership candidates.

- Examine all practices, policies, and procedures through a lens of cultural proficiency toward intersectionality and its impact on leadership development.

- Recognize and respond to the stereotypical practices of assigning women of color and indigenous women in roles that limit leadership development and career advancement.

- Be conscious and responsive to stereotypes and perceptions of indigenous women and women of color in the workplace.

The voices of retreat participants resounded with a collective harmonic sound, advocating for the health of the families they are hired to represent and holding up the futures of the thousands of children they advocate for on a daily basis. Leaders (men and women) must support of the breadth of experience and knowledge that indigenous women and women of color bring to the table to reconceptualize the mental models and dismissive actions currently in play in educational leadership.

 Looking Through the Window

As you examine policies and practices of your district, are there those that require you to give up an aspect of who you are to connect, succeed, and belong in the organization? What might be some aspects of your identity you find you have to temper, hide, or dismiss in order to feel you belong in the organization? As a leader, in what ways do you ensure that staff, students, and families do not have to give up who they are to connect, succeed, and belong in the school or district?

_____

_____

_____

_____

_____

# CHAPTER 6

# Recommending Men's Actions as Allies, Advocates, and Mentors

*Being a feminist means believing that every woman should be able to use her voice and pursue her potential, and that women and men should all work together to take down barriers and end the biases that still hold women back.*

—Melinda Gates (2019, p. 7)

 LOOKING in the MIRROR

Does Melinda Gates's definition of *feminism* align with your values and belief system as an educational leader? On a continuum from creating barriers, intentionally or unintentionally, to being an ally, advocate, and mentor, where are you? As an educational leader, female or male, where do you see yourself mentoring women as educational leaders? What are some actions, beyond traditional introductions and networking, you have taken to interrupt gender inequities in educational leadership? What might be some specific actions you can take to support and strengthen men on their journeys toward mentoring, promoting, and supporting women leaders? In what ways will you measure your success as an advocate for women educational leaders?

## MEN AS INTERRUPTERS, ALLIES, ADVOCATES, AND MENTORS

This book is written by women and about women, but it is not written solely *for* women. Gender bias cannot be interrupted by women alone. We seek the partnership of our male colleagues as allies, mentors, and bias interrupters. President Barack Obama's final press conference in 2014 interrupted the status quo as he selected inquiries from female journalists for the eight final media questions of his year-end press conference. Although some may dispute this intentional move as exclusive to the majority culture, others will applaud this act as a public and visible bias interrupter by a national leader from the highest office in the United States. Male leaders at every level have the opportunity and the responsibility to counter and disrupt biases. The advancement of gender equality requires awareness, advocacy, and actions as we confront the realities of gender inequities.

As part of the research for this book, we identified seven male educational leaders who we observed to challenge stereotypes, confront bias, and leverage their own expertise and privilege to benefit women as leaders. Unfortunately, we found we could not develop a list of dozens. As a matter of fact, we struggled to identify those male leaders that we and other successful female educational leaders have observed as intentional in their promotion and advocacy of women leaders. We have worked with and for many *great guys*, but we were seeking those that we identified as intentional promoters of women. We listened to these men's stories and their intentionality to disrupt predictability within their educational institutions as we sought to discover commonalities in their leadership approaches.

The following excerpts are the essence of each story we heard.

### Eduardo: Latino, Gay Male

Multiple perspectives come naturally to Eduardo. He was raised by strong Latinas. He understands that his perspective as the leader must be minimized in order to allow other perspectives to be heard and acknowledged. He was not nor is he intimidated by strong females and recognizes that more women at the table increases the likelihood of thoughtful, inclusive perspectives and decisions.

### Matteo: Italian, Straight Male

Matteo is intentional in his leadership to ensure that his executive cabinet has a balanced voice. He expanded his circle to include women through mentoring and hiring practices. He has a history of being at the table with White men and challenges himself to find women, to include women of color. He recognizes the barrier of men thinking like men and thus visualizing men in leadership positions. His intention is to alter that vision and create procedures for men to visualize women and the impact that the presence of women on the leadership team makes in an organization.

## Ray: African American, Straight Male

Ray strategically mentors women to become leaders. He taps women for leadership roles and recognizes they are not part of the clique or pathway to leadership. He is very aware of the barriers that women of color encounter and seeks to reduce the barriers in his organization. He specifically notes the unique barriers of Black women and the perceptions of them as aggressive and how they're often referred to as "angry Black women." Ray recognizes that many women of color face the additional burden of having to prove themselves by being overly prepared and overly worked without sweating, crying, or complaining. He works to overcome systems barriers such as *men will win at all costs* and *loyalty is the number-one value of the district!* He is very conscious of the additional roles that women play in their homes and responds using a gender equity lens. He encourages women not to be okay with being the *only one* and to mentor others for leadership roles. Ray advises women of sexual harassment situations to call it out, name it, and *do not go quietly!*

> *He encourages women not to be okay with being the only one and to mentor others for leadership roles.*

## Joe: African American, Straight Male

Joe identifies his strong relationship with his mother and her leadership in the home as a reason for his attention to the values of women in leadership. He models that relationship with his wife. He is accustomed to strong women in leadership roles in his homelife and workplace. As a Black male, he relates to the barriers that women confront based on stereotypes and the arrogance of the dominant culture. He has observed others prejudge and pass over women as if they are invisible. This is an experience that he recognizes as a Black man. He has observed males step to the front of the room with confidence, while women have to develop strategies and finesse, even though their competence levels are as high or higher than males. He strategically advocates in the hiring process for the woman candidate in a male-dominated position based on qualification and style. He has found women leaders to be nonjudgmental, patient, steady, and collaborative.

> *He has observed males step to the front of the room with confidence, while women have to develop strategies and finesse, even though their competence levels are as high or higher than males.*

## Bob: White, Straight Male

Bob intentionally mentors women as leaders. He works to convince them of their capabilities. He assures a workplace that does not necessitate a choice between family and work. He honors the importance of career and home and strategically models this through values and actions. He holds reasonable expectations of all employees and recognizes that woman leaders may

> *I recognized the concept of "his turn" and realized I had never heard "her turn."*

have different realities than their male colleagues. Bob works to ensure that his decisions, from the mundane to policy, are thoughtful and balanced. His values for gender equity stem from a male mentor, early in Bob's career, who advocated for balanced perspectives and the necessity to seek diverse leaders. Bob said, *I recognized the concept of "his turn" and realized I had never heard "her turn."* He made it his responsibility to eliminate that disparity on his watch.

## Randall: White, Straight Male

Randall believes that nothing can get in the way when leaders are focused on a clear vision and goals. He encourages women to lead, even if they think they are not ready or capable. He supports women in cohorts, women networks, collaborative organizations, and formal and informal relationships to serve as mentors and coaches to other women leaders inside and outside the organization. Randall states, *Gender inequity is no longer an option.* As a White male, he uses his privilege to assist boards and other policy makers to examine equitable hiring practices and compensation. Randall says, *White males must mentor up the system so other males know and understand the contributions women will make and how the organization will benefit from their perspectives, experiences, and leadership skills.*

> *White males must mentor up the system so other males know and understand the contributions women will make and how the organization will benefit from their perspectives, experiences, and leadership skills.*

## Jason: White, Gay Male

Jason is intentional about his promotion and sponsorship of women in leadership. He has observed women standing in line and waiting their turn, in contrast to men pushing themselves forward into leadership roles. As a leader, he is constantly on the lookout for *who is in the room* and encourages women to prepare, apply, take a risk, and recognize their competence. Jason recognizes that traditional roles of the female educator are not generally pathways to executive leadership roles. Jason's goal is to alter those pathways toward math, science, technology, and secondary-level leadership roles that lead to executive leadership positions. Jason conducts leadership training academies and invites women who may not see themselves as leaders—yet have demonstrated their leadership capabilities—to join the group.

### Reflection

As a male reading the summary comments from the men we interviewed, where are you on the continuum of support? As a female leader, what are your reactions and insights as you read the summaries?

## RECOMMENDING ACTIONS FOR ALL MALES

From the focused interviews and conversations with allies, mentors, and advocates, we found commonalities and themes in the comments and responses. We offer the following targeted actions that surfaced from our interviews for all males:

- **Mentor women with intention and purpose.** Women are less likely than men to receive targeted mentoring that promotes advancement in their careers and opens professional doors for them. Valuable relationships are instrumental to the success of women in leadership. Women who seek positions of influence need experienced mentors from the top of the organization, particularly in positions where women are in the minority. We encourage men to seek out women within the organization to mentor. We provide caution of the traditional hierarchical mentor relationship, which can create a "heroic rescuer" to the female protégée (Johnson & Smith, 2018). Belle Rose Ragins and Kathy Kram's research (2007) substantiates that mentorships with the greatest impact are mutual in nature. Both mentor and mentee benefit from the relationship. We all have a responsibility to lead and learn. Although mentors generally have more experience, female mentees bring insights to the table that can be mutually beneficial to the relationship and ultimately to the promotion of gender equity and inclusion within the organization. Mentoring benefits the recipient as well as the mentor. Hearing a female's workplace experience is a powerful way to truly understand the reality and relevancy of gender bias. High-impact mentorships between men and women have distinctive characteristics to include mutual listening and affirmation, humility, shared power, and an extended range of outcomes (Johnson & Smith, 2018.) The extended range of mentoring outcomes is strengthened from solely navigating professional advancements to conversations that cover issues such as the imposter syndrome, gender identity, work–family challenges, and resiliency. When women say they are *not ready, not prepared, or not qualified,* allow them to see themselves through a different lens as perhaps lacking confidence but not competence.

- **Value the multiple perspectives, talents, capabilities, and voices of women.** Gender-diverse teams make for richer and more impactful leadership teams. A socially responsible organization with a diversity of perspectives and opinions is a healthy one for every individual. As you grow your talent pipeline and pathways for women, the organization thrives. The voice of the female leader will offer a diverse perspective and will also foster innovation, greater profitability, and creativity. Therefore, male team members must recognize and ensure that the voice of the woman is uninterrupted, maximized, and validated for her contribution. Set the goal of listening to women and the nuances of gender diversity and resist the urge to interrupt with solutions or opinions. When different points of view are brought together, narrow perspectives are less likely to prevail. Women will become more motivated when male leaders are explicit about their disapproval of gender biases that result in leadership imbalance. The voices of women will broaden the understanding of the challenges, experiences, and unique contributions of the woman in leadership.

- **Recognize and seek to eliminate biases in the workplace.** Gender bias can be described as an unintentional mental association stemming from tradition, perceptions, norms, values, culture, and/or experience. When we hear the titles Superintendent, Chief Business Official, Chief Executive Officer, President, or Chief Technology Officer, the image that surfaces is often of a male. Although diversity training within any organization is a useful tool, it is only the beginning. Good intentions, vague goals, or an absence of clear outcomes will not lead to gender parity. A commitment to clearly stated outcomes as meaningful metrics of success, aligned with the training, will establish the desired results of gender diversity. Superintendent and cabinet-level leaders take opportunities to demonstrate actions that reflect the given values of the organization. Difficult and courageous conversations led by the leader are essential in the building of the pipeline toward gender equity. The male leader must demonstrate and model fair treatment, as well as hold others accountable. Male leaders are required to speak up even when the female is not in the room. Whether it is in the boardroom or the locker room, the expectations are the same. The leader who publicly denounces sexism and consistently models equity with every action is one who ensures a confident and comfortable workplace for all employees. When a woman is called bossy, bitchy, aggressive, shrill, or overly ambitious, mindful leaders request and expect specific examples that lend themselves to these descriptors. Male allies are prepared to challenge the assumptions and discuss the contrasting characteristics of a male in a similar scenario. The feeling of belonging is one privilege that the male educational leader often enjoys as an unearned advantage. Organizational leaders must seek ways to ensure that the female employee also enjoys a sense of belonging and connectedness, thereby reducing and eliminating unearned advantages.

- **Advocate for women in securing and sustaining leadership positions.** Although women comprise half the workforce in the United States, they are vastly underrepresented in positions of executive leadership. Unconscious and institutional blind spots can be attributed to the stubborn persistence of gender inequities in the hiring practices. The Tools of Cultural Proficiency are the foundational components to be used in all aspects of the organization and most certainly in the human resources departments as they determine who gets through the door. The Cultural Proficiency Framework provides the following guidelines:

- Review and revise the screening, interviewing, and hiring practices of the organization, eliminating barriers for female candidates. Identify any deterrents to females "getting in" because of gender.

- Examine all documents and procedures with a culturally proficient lens, with an emphasis on succession, planning, and promotion.

- Revisit career pathways available to women. The traditional female pathway of elementary teacher, curriculum specialist, or elementary principal is generally not the road to the superintendency. How can you create pathways that encourage women to fill the roles that are pipelines to executive leadership positions that have been historically filled by male leaders?

- Provide leadership training, mock interviews, and counseling for candidates.

- Conduct an in-depth compensation study to determine if there are financial discrepancies as a result of gender discrimination. Are men and women compensated equitably? Women are less likely than men to negotiate for salaries and benefits. Women incur extreme financial losses due to their avoidance of negotiations. In *What Works: Gender Equality by Design* (2018), Iris Bohnet finds that when women act more like men and "lean in," they get pushed back. Bohnet recommends that organizations train managers to counteract their biases and that women be encouraged to bring someone to assist and support them with negotiations.

- **Include male participation in family-friendly policies.** This will eliminate perceptions that these policies are to accommodate women only, thereby continuing to perpetuate the myth that the home is solely women's work.

- **Recognize and value the unique challenges of the woman in her homelife.** Sally Blount, Dean of the Kellogg School of Business at Northwestern College (2017), labels the struggle between home and work for the female leader as the *mid-career marathon*. Women are torn between work and the stressors of homelife. They are often forced by the organization to make choices that disqualify them from positions of leadership. Motherhood creates false assumptions that women are suddenly less competent or less dedicated to their workplace. Male leaders can be of tremendous assistance by modeling realistic expectations and demonstrating their understanding of the traditional female role in the home. Men can clearly demonstrate their understanding that, in most cases, the workplace is not a level playing field. On average, women in the US still do twice the housework and twice as much child care as men. The sleep of women is two-and-a-half times more likely to be interrupted as they care for others. Avoid telling mothers, *I don't know how you do it all*, which—although well intended—may be a signal that they should not be at work. Males sharing their own stories and the time they devote to family as working fathers provides mothers with permission to devote time to their family without guilt (Blount, 2017).

- **Examine board policy for issues of gender inequity.** Address unique challenges of women as leaders in board policy and procedures to include job shares, maternity leave, parental leaves, breastfeeding mothers, schedule adjustments, flexible hours, and gradual return programs to address attrition and advancement as women balance family and career. When board policy does not include or eliminates the unique accommodations designed for women, it becomes a barrier to success for all employees.

- **Establish and encourage women's networks and collaboratives.** Men have historically been admitted into executive training programs in higher numbers than women. Networks are critical to the acceleration of a woman's career. Equity leaders, allies, advocates, and mentors can support the woman in educational leadership using the following intentional networking strategies:

  - Encourage women to attend, join, and connect with other women in formal and informal ways.
  - Form a male advocacy group and provide platforms for men to demonstrate their commitment to gender equity. A male ally group can further clarify roles in incorporating gender-supportive behaviors on the job. Provide opportunities for women to benefit from male and female networks. As women work to expand networking opportunities, they must visualize beyond the golf course to forums that are inclusive and welcoming.
  - Realize and recognize that men's uses of various platforms (e.g., attendance of women's conferences, coauthoring with female leaders in leadership journals, walking in women's movement rallies) to demonstrate their commitment to gender

equity are symbolic, intentional, public, and critical to women leaders. This transparent display of intentional inclusion strengthens the commitment of the organization to gender equity.

The dialogue on gender equity involves everyone. This is not women speaking to women about women. When a workplace is gender biased, all employees suffer. We invite and encourage you to be part of the conversation. We appreciate and acknowledge the allies, advocates, and mentors who are engaging in gender equity efforts and are relentlessly advocating for an intentional voice at the table for every educational leader.

 Looking Through the Window······························

As you look through the window of your organization, in what ways have male leaders in your district intentionally interrupted gender inequities? What are the actions that have been taken to reveal gender blindness and biases within the organization? What are some actions taken to support gender equity by the male allies, mentors, and advocates?

_____

_____

_____

_____

_____

# CHAPTER 7

# Leading While Female

## A Call for Action

*Women have become more conscious of their own strengths and capacities to make a difference in the world; consequently, they have turned their attention to the next generation.*

—Lambert and Gardner (2009, p. 149)

 **LOOKING in the MIRROR**

Female and male colleagues: As you hold the mirror for this final glance at yourself, what are you noticing? What do you see that you did not see prior to reading this book? What might be some things you'll say to the "next-generation" leader as a result of your learning? How do you describe your strengths and capacities to make a difference in the world, as Lambert and Gardner mentioned in their opening quote?

_____

_____

_____

_____

_____

## WHAT WILL IT TAKE?

Now that you know what you know about gender inequities and imbalances in educational leadership, to what actions are you willing to commit? Designing a gender equity plan is the focus of this chapter. Lambert and Gardner (2009), researchers in women leadership, remind us that momentary acts of courage, such as in wartime, are critically important to our nation but may not alter or sustain significant social injustices. The researchers write about a leadership perspective called *courage and passion: Courage to promote universal values; Passion that ignites and sustains creativity and action* (p. 79).

Educational leaders must display their courage and passion for equitable practices. Michele Obama (2018), former US First Lady, gave us clear directions:

> *Let's invite one another in. Maybe then we can begin to fear less, make fewer wrong assumptions, to let go of the biases and stereotypes that unnecessarily divide us.* (p. 421)

The courage to confront social injustices, especially in public education, requires an action plan to sustain inquiry, learning, leading, and growth. Now is the time for females to lead and take action that is inclusive of their mentors, female and male, for gender equity in educational leadership. If we do not actively—with courage and passion—move forward with specific action plans, our pipelines will narrow even further, and we will betray our next generation of prospective female leaders. Jennifer Brown (2016), an inclusion workplace specialist, reports a perception gap of gender equality. She says that *75% of millennial women report that society has to do more to advance workplace equality; only 57% of millennial men agree* (p. 114). In considering the opinions of young men who observed their career moms face challenges in the workplace and are aware of the gender inequities in the workplace, Brown wonders if they will become partners in action plans for change, or if they will continue to recruit, hire, and mentor mostly White men. Brown said she heard this statement repeatedly by White, male human resource managers: *I hire the best person for the job. I don't see gender or race* (p. 122). But we can no longer afford this cultural blindness, sometimes called unconscious bias, to dominate hiring practices for schools and districts.

> *Now that you know what you know about gender inequities and imbalances in educational leadership, to what actions are you willing to commit?*

### What's a Woman to Do?

When we started writing this book, we wanted to make sure we could offer emerging female leaders and experienced female leaders some specific actions they could take to overcome barriers and move forward in achieving their career goals as educational leaders. Our search for actions led us to conduct face-to-face interviews with women and men, to have text and phone interviews with them, and to study research reports focused on theories of feminism, personal narratives, and overcoming gender inequities. From these data, we developed patterns of actions and themes of behaviors to help us determine suggestions we might make for our colleagues on their gender equity journeys. We recommend the following actions for women in different points on their pathways.

## To Emerging Female Leaders

- **Know your "why."** Leading schools and districts is not easy work. Using the lens of equity, access, and inclusion helps focus your leadership actions on creating conditions for all students to achieve success at levels higher than ever before. What's your response when an interview panel member asks, *Why do you want to do this work and what difference will you make?*

- **Prepare yourself well for the job you want.** Know your career goals and the path that will take you there. Do you have the educational background you'll need for the ultimate job you want? Don't wait until you're applying for your dream job to start your doctoral studies.

- **Locate a mentor.** Who knows the path to the goal you've set? Who is an ally for equity and diversity? Who knows your strengths, advocates for your growth, and provides feedback to help develop your confidence? Who knows about issues of gender inequity and has learned to mentor within the system for the need and value to hire women leaders? When you find the person who knows you and the system, you'll have found an excellent mentor.

- **Search for and join a network.** Seek a formal gathering of women educational leaders and join their organization. Ask experienced leaders what you should know. Pay attention to keynote speakers and listen for their barriers and support systems. Listen for the narratives they tell. Ask, *What lessons are there for me?*

- **Wait for the "match."** Say yes when you've found the job that aligns with your leadership values and beliefs. Have the confidence not to doubt your competence.

- **Work on the Work.** Professional learning is lifelong learning. Don't wait for the right job to come along. Continue to read, study, facilitate, write, and build your confidence. Know what you need to know!

- **Dress the part and suit yourself.** Yes, dress for the job; and let the interviewers know who you are by the way you dress. You can do both. Just know that if an organization expects or requires you to dress in a way that denies who you are, you may need to look for an organization that values who you are. You do not need to take on the stereotypical traits of the male leader to be successful. Who you are as a woman is your greatest strength.

- **Know the numbers and the district well.** Apply or stay in a district that you know well and in which you are prepared to make a difference in your field. Examine hiring practices for equitable and accessible priorities. Ask, *Who are we?* and *Are we who we say we are?* and look for data aligned with vision.

- **Be a champion for equity, access, and diversity.** Advocate for and insist on equitable practices throughout the organization. Assess cultural knowledge of employees you supervise.

- **Ensure the "only one" experience is rare or history.** If you find yourself to be the extraordinary or the exception, work to ensure that is not the future of the organization. Take part in the hiring process and give feedback and input to ensure that diversity of candidates is top priority.

- **Honor and manage the various needs for flexibility of work hours.** Lead the organization in recognizing the barriers that were outlined in Chapter 5 that are unique to the female leader. Speak up when contracts, procedures, or policies are being adopted or revised that do not take into account family needs, such as breastfeeding, flexible hours, job shares, and family leaves.

- **Expect and adapt to the changing needs of a diverse workplace.** Be the example for the emerging leaders to follow.

- **Organize and institutionalize support functions to overcome systemic oppression.** Appoint data warriors to continuously collect and analyze data in search of indicators of unconscious barrier-building policies or procedures. For example, who knows how many women of color have left the organization within the past three years and the reasons for their departure? What might the data indicate? What assumptions might surface about support systems for women of color? Open the system for assessment, analyses, and support.

- **Mentor emerging female leaders with intention.** Recognize that the women who come after you are key to changing the culture of the organization. Welcome them and be there to guide, mentor, and leverage networks for their success. Recognize that the future of an organization is your responsibility and privilege.

## PLAN YOUR ACTION

If you are willing to use your courage and passion for equity, we offer you a Personal/District Gender Equity Action Plan in Table 7.1. This action plan template is focused on outcomes for gender equity and is dependent on identifying benchmarks/indicators for success.

**TABLE 7.1** Gender Equity Action Plan

| School/District<br>_Gender Equity Action Plan_ |
| --- |
| **Our School/District Vision:** |
| **Our School/District Mission:** |
| **Current Reality and Rationale** (Assessment data [_and other information/observations_] to describe gender inequities to be addressed.) |
| **Outcomes** (What is it we want to accomplish? What is it you want educators to know and be able to do so that gender equity can be achieved at high levels?) |
| **Goal One** (_Use SMART criteria*_: What goals will we need to establish to reach those Outcomes? To what extent are these Goals aligned with our Vision/Mission?) |
| **Goal Two** |
| **Goal Three** |

(_Continued_)

**Table 7.1** (Continued)

| Equity Action Steps (Using the following Five Essential Elements, what actions will we take to reach our goals?) | Person(s) responsible: (Positions, not names) | Resources: (Materials and/or personnel) | Timeline: (When will we benchmark?) | Funding: |
|---|---|---|---|---|
| Assessing cultural knowledge | | | | |
| Valuing diversity | | | | |
| Managing the dynamics of diversity | | | | |

Adapting to diversity

Institutionalizing cultural knowledge

**Evaluation and Indicators of Success** (For reducing and eliminating gender inequities toward achieving goal: How will we measure success? What will we use as benchmarks of success?)

*SMART GOALS

**Specific** = Who, what, when, where, which, why?

**Measurable** = Concrete criteria for measuring success: How much, how many, how will we know?

**Attainable** = Develop knowledge, skills, attitudes, and resources to attain our goals: What do we need to be successful?

**Realistic** = Is our goal high enough, and are we willing to work hard enough to reach it?

**Timely, Tangible** = What is our sense of urgency? Can we see it and hear it and feel it and know when we have reached our goal/outcome?

## Use the Gender Equity for Education Leadership Rubric

To assist you with your action planning, we designed the Rubric for Creating Culturally Proficient Responses to Gender Equity, found in Table 7.2. The actions provided in the rubric are aligned with the Five Essential Elements for Cultural Proficiency. A national panel of gender equity experts developed the actions in this rubric. Take a few minutes and read it from the left side to the right side. The headings across the top showing the Continuum are presented in a collapsed version, which is different from the manner you may have experienced in other Cultural Proficiency books.

**TABLE 7.2**  Rubric for Creating Culturally Proficient Responses for Gender Equity

| Essential Elements: Action for Gender Equity  | Actions informed by negative assumptions, stereotypes, and barriers for sustaining gender inequities | Actions informed by positive assumptions, Guiding Principles, and values in support of achieving and sustaining gender equity | |
| --- | --- | --- | --- |
| | **PITFALLS:** Cultural Destructiveness Cultural Incapacity Cultural Blindness | **PIPELINES:** Cultural Precompetence Cultural Competence | **PATHWAYS:** Cultural Proficiency |
| **Assess cultural knowledge:** Make the effort to be inclusive of people whose viewpoints and experiences are different from yours. These values will enrich conversations, decision-making, and problem solving. | Leaders: <br>• Ignore or defend inequity data that has the effect of maintaining status quo; <br>• Structure meetings with little or no opportunity to hear diverse voices and opinions; <br>• Resist changes that aid in recruitment of women in leadership; <br>• Include token voices into multicultural meetings to meet compliance; <br>• Assign women of color to diversity and equity leadership roles that have limited influence or power. | Leaders: <br>• Conduct inquiries to determine extent of gender inequities; <br>• Actively recruit highly qualified women and women of color as leadership candidates; <br>• Analyze interview protocols for possible biased practices. | Leaders: <br>• Collect qualitative and quantitative data regarding gender disparities; <br>• Use data to inform hiring and promote decision-making; <br>• Understand the dynamics of intersectionality and the dynamic aspects of individuals; <br>• Highlight and recognize the accomplishments of female leaders; <br>• Provide women the role of spokesperson, leader among leaders, and expert in front of colleagues; <br>• Seek and incorporate the knowledge, perspectives, and opinions of women in leadership positions; <br>• Speak up against gender-biased statements when women are not in the room. |

| Essential Elements: | PITFALLS: | PIPELINES: | PATHWAYS: |
|---|---|---|---|
| **Value diversity:** Make the effort to be inclusive of people whose viewpoints and experiences are different from yours. These values will enrich conversations, decision-making, and problem solving. | • Reinforce negative female stereotypes through media and social media;<br><br>• Defend all-male leadership appointments at school sites;<br><br>• Tolerate diversity recruitment programs as necessary to meet compliance guidelines;<br><br>• Seek to be in compliance to satisfy external or internal mandates;<br><br>• Ignore stereotypical comments;<br><br>• Direct women to pathways that do not lead to executive leadership positions. | • Actively seek and include women's perspectives, experiences, and opinions when recruiting, hiring, and supporting leaders;<br><br>• Structure meetings and forums to ensure that all voices are heard and respected;<br><br>• Have diverse representation on hiring panels;<br><br>• Speak up against gender-biased statements, especially when women are in the room;<br><br>• Acknowledge and publish the nonbinary nature of gender, gender identity, and sexual orientation;<br><br>• Acknowledge and publish the intersectionality of various cultures as a high value for identity. | • Highlight and recognize the accomplishments of female leaders;<br><br>• Provide women the role of spokesperson, leader among leaders, and expert in front of colleagues;<br><br>• Respond to stereotypes and misperceptions of women;<br><br>• Adopt policies to address the unique challenges of women, such as job shares, flexible hours, and parenting leave;<br><br>• Include male participants in family-friendly policies;<br><br>• Seek the perspectives and opinions of women in leadership positions;<br><br>• Speak up against gender-biased statements when women are not in the room. |
| **Manage dynamics of gender equity:** Manage the Dynamics of Difference—view conflict as a natural and normal process that has cultural contexts that can be understood and used in decision-making, creative problem solving, community building, and developing gender equity. | • Continue to appoint male-dominated committees to resolve policy issues or complaints;<br><br>• Deny the existence of gender inequities or systems of oppression;<br><br>• Pigeonhole women of color to serve and lead specific groups of students and staff that are usually overrepresented by women. | • Counter stereotypical images of women leaders with authentic images of successful women leaders;<br><br>• Be conscious of stereotypes and negative perceptions of women. | • Engage leaders in annual review of hiring and promotion profiles as a means of assessing progress toward equitable practices;<br><br>• Engage leaders in a continuous process of examining personal and organizational assumptions that underlie personnel actions. |

*(Continued)*

Table 7.2 (Continued)

| Essential Elements: | PITFALLS: | PIPELINES: | PATHWAYS: |
|---|---|---|---|
| **Adapt to changing environments:** Have the will to learn about others and the ability to apply others' cultural experiences and backgrounds in educational settings. | • Maintain status quo by limiting resources for innovation and new designs;<br><br>• Support current policies, practices, structures, and procedures to discourage change initiatives for adapting to new demographics. | • Create mentoring programs for women;<br><br>• Share experiences, barriers, and successes in formal and informal settings;<br><br>• "Tap" women and acknowledge their contributions and potential. | • Collect and publish annual audit data of the ethnic and gender profiles in leadership positions;<br><br>• Hold self and organization accountable for developing and promoting women to leadership roles. |
| **Institutionalize cultural knowledge:** Make learning about cultural groups and their experiences and perspectives an integral part of continuous growth and learning. | • Provide yearly audits as needed to validate current male-dominated workforce leaders;<br><br>• Celebrate success of status quo and need to avoid change forces;<br><br>• Accept "that's the way we have always done it" as a rationale for continuing the practice. | • Develop procedures in support of mentoring men and women leaders equitably;<br><br>• Examine the vision and guiding principles of the organization for language of equity. | • Promote men's ally networks that are specifically designed to support women;<br><br>• Provide mentoring programs that are formed in partnership and sponsorship;<br><br>• Publish guides for systemic changes for recruiting, hiring, and mentoring women leaders;<br><br>• Revise mission and vision statements to ensure the language of the organization reflects the values of equity. |

The column labeled *Pitfalls* brings together Cultural Destructiveness, Cultural Incapacity, and Cultural Blindness on the left side of the Cultural Proficiency Continuum into a single column. On the right side of the rubric, Cultural Precompetence and Cultural Competence shape actions for building equitable Pipelines for recruiting, hiring, and supporting qualified women, which includes women of color candidates. Pathways serve as Cultural Proficiency options for creating and sustaining a gender equity organization moving toward greater gender balance and equality.

In the column on the shaded left side, you will find the Five Essential Elements for Cultural Proficiency operationalized for gender equity actions. Read Table 7.2 across the rows to see the Pitfalls, Pipelines, and Pathways for gender equity. Please note that this rubric is *not* developmental across all rows. We encourage actions *from* anywhere on the left side *to* the right side—put another way, support actions that move leaders *from* Pitfalls *to* Pipelines and Pathways.

To what stage on the Continuum might your organizational practices and policies currently align? As you look to the right, what might be your next steps to move your personal or organizational practices and policies along?

## WHAT'S YOUR GENDER EQUITY ACTION PLAN?

Do you have the requisite courage and driving passion to make a difference about gender inequities? How much more data will it take to convince you of the dysfunction and imbalance of the system when female education leaders are not at the decision-making tables? How many more stories will you need to hear to move you to action? If you are willing to make a difference and open the pipelines and offer wider pathways for female leaders, now is the time to step forward with your commitment. What were your barriers/pitfalls? What were support factors? What are key actions for you and those you lead for moving forward?

**Women: What will you do now?**

_____

_____

_____

_____

_____

**Men: What will you do now?**

_____

_____

_____

_____

_____

We thank you for your commitment and your engagement to undo a system of gender inequities and the master narrative that sustains it. We invite you join us on our Cultural Proficiency journey and tell your counternarrative, action research story. Our hope is similar to Michelle Obama's (2018):

> _I hope to create space for other stories and other lives, to widen the pathway for who belongs and why. . . . There's power in allowing yourself to be known and heard, and in owning your unique story, in using your authentic voice. And, there's grace in being willing to know and hear others._ (p. 421)

As we close, we remind you that we dedicated this book to our daughters and granddaughters with the hope and confidence that their journeys will be impacted by the women who came before them, as were ours. Our expectation is that their unique gifts as women will be valued and recognized in their future workplaces. We have confidence that our sons and grandsons will be right by their sides, offering support and applause.

*Tell us your story. Contact us at . . .*

trudyarriaga73@gmail.com

staciestanley@gmail.com

dblindsey@aol.com

# Women in Education Leadership Retreat

## Leading While Female
*August 2018*

Note: At the WELR, women were asked to complete the phrase, *I am from . . . .* Here is our "I Am From . . ." poem. (Poem template inspired by George Ella Lyons.)

### I Am From . . . *Diversity of Our Circle*

*I am from washing off the dirt from fields of strawberries before school on Monday.*

*I am from* Bless Me, Ultima *and* Beloved.

*I am from a God that demands excellence and forgiveness, but not perfection.*

*I am from, "You can do anything . . . but you are selfish if you go back to school as a mother of three."*

*I am from, "Get a job to buy your lipstick and get a man."*

*I am from, "You should just drop out."*

*I am from a rancho, not a pueblo, without a church.*

*I am from a grandmother's house of love and acceptance.*

*I am from a teen mother's unselfish gift of giving me to my grandparents.*

*I am from, "Do your best and you can achieve anything," followed by, "Is that your best?"*

*I am from* Anne of Green Gables, Nancy Drew, *Laura Ingalls Wilder and* Goodbye, Mr. Chips.

*I am from, children should be seen and not heard.*

*I am from, "With all due respect, I'd like to see the superintendent," yet I am the superintendent.*

*I am from, "Your dad would be so proud."*

*I am from, "You can't be a female high school principal, be a middle school principal."*

*I am from, "You are not like them."*

*I am from men forgiving men more readily than women forgiving women.*

*I am from being the high school valedictorian but not understanding that to get a scholarship, I had to apply.*

*I am from, "Your mouth gets you in trouble, so just be quiet."*

*I am from, "You have to work harder than the White man to get where you'd like to be."*

*I am from parents to great-grandparents of hard work, tenacity and all things possible.*

*I am from the community where little girls did not graduate . . . but I did.*

*I am from not needing a man but having a crush on all the boys.*

*I am from a highly verbal family, which empowered me to speak.*

*I am from privilege and a responsibility to ensure "With liberty and justice for all."*

*I am from a husband who supports my aspirations and encourages me to pursue crazy adventures.*

*I am from a high school counselor who insisted I go to continuation school.*

*I am from an amazing grandmother who was the epitome of womanhood . . . a strong Black woman.*

*I am from hip-hop, Gospel and smooth jazz.*

*I am from one husband who kept me down and another who lifted me up.*

*I am from, "Why can't I be an altar boy?"*

*I am from, "How does a woman like you, control those eighth-grade boys?"*

*I am from a father's highest hope for me to be a secretary.*

*I am from three generations living together in harmony.*

*I am from growing up in a lonely Catholic Church as a Gay 5-year-old.*

*I am from a latchkey community where drugs and gangs terrorized the homes as Motown and Maya Angelou lifted our spirits.*

*I am from Oprah, Beyoncé, and Michele Obama . . . Black Girls Rock!*

*I am from my father's words, "You are better than any boy at everything."*

*I am from a family work ethic of achievement with no other option.*

*I am from, "You'll have to figure it out on your own."*

*I am from, "You are enough."*

# Resource

## Essential Questions

## CULTURAL PROFICIENCY BOOKS' ESSENTIAL QUESTIONS

| CORWIN CULTURAL PROFICIENCY BOOKS | AUTHORS OR EDITORS | FOCUS AND ESSENTIAL QUESTIONS |
|---|---|---|
| • *Cultural Proficiency: A Manual for School Leaders*, 4th ed., 2019 | • Randall B. Lindsey<br><br>• Raymond D. Terrell<br><br>• Kikanza Nuri-Robins<br><br>• Delores B. Lindsey | • This book is an introduction to Cultural Proficiency. The book provides readers with extended discussion of each of the Tools and the historical Framework for diversity work.<br><br>• What is Cultural Proficiency? How does Cultural Proficiency differ from other responses to diversity?<br><br>• In what ways do I incorporate the Tools of Cultural Proficiency into my practice?<br><br>• How do I use the resources and activities to support professional learning?<br><br>• How do I identify Barriers to student learning?<br><br>• How do the Guiding Principles and Essential Elements support better education for students?<br><br>• What does the inside-out process mean for me as an educator?<br><br>• How do I foster challenging conversations with colleagues?<br><br>• How do I extend my own learning? |
| • *Culturally Proficient Instruction: A Guide for People Who Teach*, 3rd ed., 2012 | • Kikanza Nuri-Robins<br><br>• Randall B. Lindsey<br><br>• Delores B. Lindsey<br><br>• Raymond D. Terrell | • This book focuses on the Five Essential Elements and can be helpful to anyone in an instructional role. This book can be used as a workbook for a study group.<br><br>• What does it mean to be a culturally proficient instructor?<br><br>• How do I incorporate Cultural Proficiency into a school's learning community processes?<br><br>• How do we move from "mindset" or "mental model" to a set of practices in our school? |

*(Continued)*

(Continued)

| CORWIN CULTURAL PROFICIENCY BOOKS | AUTHORS OR EDITORS | FOCUS AND ESSENTIAL QUESTIONS |
|---|---|---|
| | | • How does my "cultural story" support being effective as an educator with my students?<br>• In what ways might we apply the Maple View story to our learning community?<br>• In what ways can I integrate the Guiding Principles of Cultural Proficiency with my own values about learning and learners?<br>• In what ways do the Essential Elements as standards inform and support our work with the Common Core State Standards (CCSS)?<br>• How do I foster challenging conversations with colleagues?<br>• How do I extend my own learning? |
| • *The Culturally Proficient School: An Implementation Guide for School Leaders,* 2nd ed., 2013 | • Randall B. Lindsey<br>• Laraine M. Roberts<br>• Franklin CampbellJones | • This book guides readers to examine their school as a cultural organization and to design and implement approaches to dialogue and inquiry.<br>• In what ways do Cultural Proficiency and school leadership help me close achievement gaps?<br>• What are the communication skills I need to master to support my colleagues when focusing on achievement gap topics?<br>• How do "transactional" and "transformational" changes differ and inform closing achievement gaps in my school or district?<br>• How do I foster challenging conversations with colleagues?<br>• How do I extend my own learning? |
| • *Culturally Proficient Coaching: Supporting Educators to Create Equitable Schools,* 2007 | • Delores B. Lindsey<br>• Richard S. Martinez<br>• Randall B. Lindsey | • This book aligns the Essential Elements with Costa and Garmston's Cognitive Coaching model. The book provides coaches, teachers, and administrators a personal guidebook with protocols and maps for conducting conversations that shift thinking in support of all students achieving at levels higher than ever before.<br>• What are the coaching skills I need to work with diverse student populations?<br>• In what ways do the Tools of Cultural Proficiency and Cognitive Coaching's States of Mind support me in addressing achievement issues in my school?<br>• How do I foster challenging conversations with colleagues?<br>• How do I extend my own learning? |

| CORWIN CULTURAL PROFICIENCY BOOKS | AUTHORS OR EDITORS | FOCUS AND ESSENTIAL QUESTIONS |
|---|---|---|
| • *Culturally Proficient Inquiry: A Lens for Identifying and Examining Educational Gaps,* 2008 | • Randall B. Lindsey<br>• Stephanie M. Graham<br>• R. Chris Westphal Jr.<br>• Cynthia L. Jew | • This book uses protocols for gathering and analyzing student achievement and access data. Rubrics for gathering and analyzing data about educator practices are also presented. A CD accompanies the book for easy downloading and use of the data protocols.<br>• How do we move from the "will" to educate all children to actually developing our "skills" and doing so?<br>• In what ways do we use the various forms of student achievement data to inform educator practice?<br>• In what ways do we use access data (e.g., suspensions, absences, enrollment in special education or gifted classes) to inform schoolwide practices?<br>• How do we use the four rubrics to inform educator professional learning?<br>• How do I foster challenging conversations with colleagues?<br>• How do I extend my own learning? |
| • *Culturally Proficient Leadership: The Personal Journey Begins Within,* 2nd ed., 2018 | • Raymond D. Terrell<br>• Eloise K. Terrell<br>• Delores B. Lindsey<br>• Randall B. Lindsey | • This book guides the reader through the development of a cultural autobiography as a means to becoming an increasingly effective leader in our diverse society. The book is an effective tool for use by leadership teams.<br>• How did I develop my attitudes about others' cultures?<br>• When I engage in intentional cross-cultural communication, how can I use those experiences to heighten my effectiveness?<br>• In what ways can I grow into being a culturally proficient leader?<br>• How do I foster challenging conversations with colleagues?<br>• How do I extend my own learning? |
| • *Culturally Proficient Learning Communities: Confronting Inequities Through Collaborative Curiosity,* 2009 | • Delores B. Lindsey<br>• Linda D. Jungwirth<br>• Jarvis V. N. C. Pahl<br>• Randall B. Lindsey | • This book provides readers a lens through which to examine the purpose, the intentions, and the progress of learning communities to which they belong or wish to develop. School and district leaders are provided protocols, activities, and rubrics to engage in actions focused on the intersection of race, ethnicity, gender, social class, sexual orientation and identity, faith, and ableness with the disparities in student achievement.<br>• What is necessary for a learning community to become a "culturally proficient learning community"? |

*(Continued)*

(Continued)

| CORWIN CULTURAL PROFICIENCY BOOKS | AUTHORS OR EDITORS | FOCUS AND ESSENTIAL QUESTIONS |
|---|---|---|
| | | • What is organizational culture, and how do I describe my school's culture in support of equity and access? |
| | | • What are *curiosity* and *collaborative curiosity*, and how do I foster them at my school or district? |
| | | • How will "breakthrough questions" enhance my work as a learning community member and leader? |
| | | • How do I foster challenging conversations with colleagues? |
| | | • How do I extend my own learning? |
| • *The Cultural Proficiency Journey: Moving Beyond Ethical Barriers Toward Profound School Change,* 2010 | • Franklin CampbellJones <br> • Brenda CampbellJones <br> • Randall B. Lindsey | • This book explores Cultural Proficiency as an ethical construct. It makes transparent the connection between values, assumptions, and beliefs as well as observable behavior, making change possible and sustainable. The book is appropriate for book study teams. |
| | | • In what ways does *moral consciousness* inform and support my role as an educator? |
| | | • How do a school's "core values" become reflected in assumptions held about students? |
| | | • What steps do I take to ensure that my school and I understand any low expectations we might have? |
| | | • How do we recognize that our low expectations serve as ethical barriers? |
| | | • How do I foster challenging conversations with colleagues? |
| | | • How do I extend my own learning? |
| • *Culturally Proficient Education: An Assets-Based Response to Conditions of Poverty,* 2010 | • Randall B. Lindsey <br> • Michelle S. Karns <br> • Keith Myatt | • This book is written for educators to learn how to identify and develop the strengths of students from low-income backgrounds. It is an effective learning community resource to promote reflection and dialogue. |
| | | • What are "assets" that students bring to school? |
| | | • How do we operate from an "assets-based" perspective? |
| | | • What are my and my school's expectations about students from low-income and impoverished backgrounds? |
| | | • How do I foster challenging conversations with colleagues? |
| | | • How do I extend my own learning? |

| CORWIN CULTURAL PROFICIENCY BOOKS | AUTHORS OR EDITORS | FOCUS AND ESSENTIAL QUESTIONS |
|---|---|---|
| • *Culturally Proficient Collaboration: Use and Misuse of School Counselors*, 2011 | • Diana L. Stephens<br>• Randall B. Lindsey | • This book uses the lens of Cultural Proficiency to frame the American School Counseling Association's performance standards and the Education Trust's Transforming School Counseling Initiative as means for addressing issues of access and equity in schools in collaborative school leadership teams.<br>• How do counselors fit into achievement-related conversations with administrators and teachers?<br>• What is the "new role" for counselors?<br>• How does this "new role" differ from existing views of school counselor?<br>• What is the role of site administrators in this new role of school counselor?<br>• How do I foster challenging conversations with colleagues?<br>• How do I extend my own learning? |
| • *A Culturally Proficient Society Begins in School: Leadership for Equity*, 2011 | • Carmella S. Franco<br>• Maria G. Ott<br>• Darline P. Robles | • This book frames the life stories of three superintendents through the lens of Cultural Proficiency. The reader is provided the opportunity to design or modify his or her own leadership for equity plan.<br>• In what ways is the role of school superintendent related to equity issues?<br>• Why is this topic important to me as a superintendent or aspiring superintendent?<br>• What are the leadership characteristics of a culturally proficient school superintendent?<br>• How do I foster challenging conversations with colleagues?<br>• How do I extend my own learning? |
| • *The Best of Corwin: Equity*, 2012 | • Randall B. Lindsey | • This edited book provides a range of perspectives of published chapters from prominent authors on topics of equity, access, and diversity. It is designed for use by school study groups.<br>• In what ways do these readings support our professional learning?<br>• How might I use these readings to engage others in learning conversations to support all students learning and all educators educating all students? |

*(Continued)*

(Continued)

| CORWIN CULTURAL PROFICIENCY BOOKS | AUTHORS OR EDITORS | FOCUS AND ESSENTIAL QUESTIONS |
|---|---|---|
| • *Culturally Proficient Practice: Supporting Educators of English Learning Students,* 2012 | • Reyes L. Quezada<br>• Delores B. Lindsey<br>• Randall B. Lindsey | • This book guides readers to apply the Five Essential Elements of Cultural Competence to their individual practice and their school's approaches to equity. The book works well for school study groups.<br>• In what ways do I foster support for the education of English-learning students?<br>• How can I use action research strategies to inform my practice with English-learning students?<br>• In what ways might this book support all educators in our district or school?<br>• How do I foster challenging conversations with colleagues?<br>• How do I extend my own learning? |
| • *A Culturally Proficient Response to LGBT Communities: A Guide for Educators,* 2013 | • Randall B. Lindsey<br>• Richard Diaz<br>• Kikanza Nuri-Robins<br>• Raymond D. Terrell<br>• Delores B. Lindsey | • This book guides the reader to understand sexual orientation in a way that provides for the educational needs of all students. The reader explores values, behaviors, policies, and practices that impact lesbian, gay, bisexual, and transgender (LGBT) students, educators, and parents or guardians.<br>• How do I foster support for LGBT colleagues, students, and parents or guardians?<br>• In what ways does our school represent a value for LGBT members?<br>• How can I create a safe environment for all students to learn?<br>• To what extent is my school an environment where it is safe for the adults to be open about their sexual orientation?<br>• How do I reconcile my attitudes toward religion and sexuality with my responsibilities as a preK–12 educator?<br>• How do I foster challenging conversations with colleagues?<br>• How do I extend my own learning? |
| • *Opening Doors: An Implementation Template for Cultural Proficiency,* 2016 | • Trudy T. Arriaga<br>• Randall B. Lindsey | • This book serves as a template for school leaders to use in determining levels of inclusiveness in their schools/districts.<br>• In what ways do I use this book to deepen my understanding of equity and inclusiveness in action?<br>• In what ways do I lead to become aware of underlying core values that limit access to students and families? |

| CORWIN CULTURAL PROFICIENCY BOOKS | AUTHORS OR EDITORS | FOCUS AND ESSENTIAL QUESTIONS |
|---|---|---|
| | | • In what ways do I lead my school/district to develop and live authentic and inclusive core values and mission statements? |
| | | • How do I extend my own learning? |
| • *Fish Out of Water: Mentoring, Managing, and Self-Monitoring People Who Don't Fit In,* 2016 | • Kikanza Nuri-Robins<br>• Lewis Bundy | • This book helps the reader manage the dynamics of difference by focusing on sustaining a healthy organizational culture using the Cultural Proficiency Continuum as a template. Strategies based on the Guiding Principles of Cultural Proficiency and the Essential Elements of Cultural Proficiency are provided for supporting both children and adults who are struggling to understand or use the cultural norms of a particular environment. A study guide is provided in the Resources so that the book can easily be used for professional development or a small-group book study. |
| | | • How do I determine the nature of diversity in this environment? |
| | | • How might I understand who is thriving in this setting and who is not? |
| | | • Are there any groups that are being targeted? |
| | | • Are the rules of the environment oppressive to any individuals or groups in the environment? |
| | | • Why are certain groups making the organizational rules for everyone? |
| | | • How might I address systems to make the environment healthier? |
| | | • What strategies are available to my colleagues and me as we seek to sustain a healthy, inclusive environment for all? |
| | | • What strategies are available to an individual who is trying to succeed in a toxic environment? |
| | | • How do I extend my own learning? |
| • *Guiding Teams to Excellence With Equity: Culturally Proficient Facilitation,* 2017 | • John Krownapple | • This book provides mental models and information for educators to develop as facilitators of professional learning and organizational change for equity in education. It also supports experienced professional developers with tools for doing their work in a culturally competent and proficient manner. This book is for organizations working to build internal capacity and sustainability for Cultural Proficiency. |
| | | • Assuming we value excellence and equity in education, why do we need Cultural Proficiency and culturally proficient facilitators of the process? |

*(Continued)*

| CORWIN CULTURAL PROFICIENCY BOOKS | AUTHORS OR EDITORS | FOCUS AND ESSENTIAL QUESTIONS |
| --- | --- | --- |
| | | • How can we use Cultural Proficiency as content (the framework) and process (the journey) to achieve excellence with equity?<br><br>• What do facilitators do in order to work with teams in a culturally proficient manner? |
| • *A Culturally Proficient Response to the Common Core: Ensuring Equity Through Professional Learning*, 2015 | • Delores B. Lindsey<br><br>• Karen M. Kearney<br><br>• Delia Estrada<br><br>• Raymond D. Terrell<br><br>• Randall B. Lindsey | • This book guides the reader to view and use the Common Core State Standards (CCSS) as a vehicle for ensuring all demographic groups of students are fully prepared for college and careers.<br><br>• In what ways do I use this book to deepen my learning about equity?<br><br>• In what ways do I use this book to deepen my learning about CCSS?<br><br>• In what ways do I use this book with colleagues to deepen our work on equity and on the CCSS?<br><br>• How can I and we use the action planning guide as an overlay for our current school planning? |
| • *Culturally Proficient Inclusive Schools: All means ALL!*, 2018 | • Delores B. Lindsey<br><br>• Jacqueline S. Thousand<br><br>• Cindy L. Jew<br><br>• Lori R. Piowlski | • This book provides responses and applications of the four Tools of Cultural Proficiency for educators who desire to create and support classrooms and schools that are inclusive and designed intentionally to educate all learners. General educators and special educators will benefit from using the Five Essential Elements and the tenets of inclusive schooling to create and sustain educational environments so that when we say *all* students, we truly mean *all*! students will achieve at levels higher than ever before.<br><br>• What might be some ways general and special educators can work collaboratively to create conditions for all students to be successful?<br><br>• In what ways does this book address issues of equity and access for all students?<br><br>• How do the four Tools of Cultural Proficiency inform the work of inclusive schooling? What's here for you?<br><br>• In what ways does the action plan template offer opportunities for you and your colleagues?<br><br>• For what are you waiting to help narrow and close equity gaps in your classroom and schools?<br><br>• How do I foster challenging conversations about inclusive education with colleagues?<br><br>• How do I extend my own learning about ways in which to facilitate inclusive learning environments? |

| CORWIN CULTURAL PROFICIENCY BOOKS | AUTHORS OR EDITORS | FOCUS AND ESSENTIAL QUESTIONS |
| --- | --- | --- |
| • *The Cultural Proficiency Manifesto: Finding Clarity Amidst the Noise,* 2017 | • Randall B. Lindsey | • This book is a call to action for educators to ensure we are creating culturally inclusive and responsive environments for our students.<br>• What are the lessons learned, the answers to equip educators to address issues of inequity?<br>• In what ways do educators use the Tools of Cultural Proficiency in listening for clarity while living amidst turmoil?<br>• What are behaviors of commitment in moving from practices of inequity to practices of equity? |
| • *Culturally Proficient Coaching: Supporting Educators to Create Equitable Schools,* 2nd. ed., 2020 | • Delores B. Lindsey<br>• Richard S. Martinez<br>• Randall B. Lindsey<br>• Keith T. Myatt | • This book aligns the Five Essential Elements with the Cognitive Coaching model. The book provides coaches, teachers, and administrators a personal guidebook with protocols and maps for conducting conversations that shift thinking in support of all students achieving at levels higher than ever before.<br>• What are the coaching skills I need in working with diverse student populations?<br>• In what ways do the Tools of Cultural Proficiency and Cognitive Coaching's States of Mind support my addressing achievement issues in my school?<br>• How do I craft challenging breakthrough questions with colleagues?<br>• How do I extend my own learning? |
| • *Leading While Female: A Culturally Proficient Response for Gender Equity,* 2020 | • Trudy T. Arriaga<br>• Stacie L. Stanley<br>• Delores B. Lindsey | • This book is a call to action for women, men, hiring managers, mentors, and sponsors to ensure we are creating gender-inclusive work environments that foster pipelines and pathways to executive leadership for women.<br>• What key factors in educational systems must shift to ensure women/female are equitably prepared to serve in executive leadership?<br>• In what ways might the Tools of Cultural Proficiency be used to support pipelines and pathways for women in executive leadership?<br>• How might the Continuum of Cultural Proficiency serve to support long-term system change?<br>• What are the opportunities and actions for men to support the opening of doors for women in executive leadership?<br>• What is my role as mentor and sponsor toward ensuring hiring disparities for women in executive leadership are eliminated? |

# Book Study Guide for *Leading While Female*

## CHAPTER 1: OWNING THE STORIES WE TELL—OUR COUNTERNARRATIVES

### Content Questions to Consider

- What is your story?
- In what ways has your gender informed your narrative as an educator?
- How has the reading of the stories of the authors assisted you in reflecting on your own story?

### Personal Reaction Questions to Consider

- What is your reaction to the intent of the book?
- What was your first reaction to the title of this book?
- In what ways did others react to the title, or did you notice?
- What is your comfort level in discussing gender inequities in educational leadership?
- What might be some narratives of gender or gender equity for your organization? Are there counternarratives?
- Now, how does the title of the book—*Leading While Female*—resonate with you?
- How might you make the time within the organization to share your story and listen to each other's stories to help guide you in the future?

## CHAPTER 2: CULTURAL PROFICIENCY—A FRAMEWORK FOR GENDER EQUITY

### Content Questions to Consider

- How might you describe the Tools of Cultural Proficiency?

- How does the *inside-out process* relate to you and your role in gender equity for educational leaders?

- Are you prepared to examine gender equity with the lens of cultural proficiency as a means to disrupt inequities?

### Personal Reaction Questions to Consider

- What is your personal reaction as you become acquainted with the Tools of Cultural Proficiency?

- What policies, practices, and procedures within your school/district might you identify that can be placed on the Continuum of Cultural Proficiency?

## CHAPTER 3: CONFRONTING AND OVERCOMING BARRIERS

### Content Questions to Consider

- What barriers within your organization might you identify that exist in regard to women in leadership?

- As you explore your human resources department, what specific barriers might exist in the Pipeline or Pathways to executive leadership positions?

- Do the actions of your organization support the stated values in the mission or vision statements within your school/district?

### Personal Reaction Questions to Consider

- Can you identify other examples of gender bias in your formative years?

- What steps will you take to disrupt gender-biased actions that lead to barriers for women in leadership?

- Do you have personal experiences that could add to the richness of the stories of the circle of men and women who shared their stories?

## CHAPTER 4: MOVING FORWARD WITH GUIDING PRINCIPLES

### Content Questions to Consider

- In what ways are the Guiding Principles consistent with your school or district's response to gender equity?
- Explain how the Guiding Principles counter the Barriers to gender equity in educational leadership.

### Personal Reaction Questions to Consider

- Are you who you say you are?
- How does the vision or mission statement within your organization clearly address the value of diversity and equity?
- Can you identify networks within your region that support, guide, and mentor women as educational leaders? How might they be strengthened?

## CHAPTER 5: UNDERSTANDING FEMINISM, IDENTITY, AND INTERSECTIONALITY—WHO AM I? WHO ARE WE?

### Content Questions to Consider

- Who are you?
- What might be some examples and evidence of stereotypical practices that "pigeonhole" women in roles that limit leadership development and career advancement?
- How does the Guiding Principle, *Diversity exists within the group identity,* help to define intersectionality?

### Personal Reaction Questions to Consider

- How does the concept of feminism personally resonate with you?
- Which voices have been left out or drowned out within your organization?
- What unique perspective do you bring to the organization?
- Do you ever have to give up an aspect of your identity to connect, succeed, or belong in the organization?

## CHAPTER 6: RECOMMENDING MEN'S ACTIONS AS ALLIES, ADVOCATES, AND MENTORS

### Content Questions to Consider

- Can you identify males in your organization who are intentional promoters of women? What do they specifically do to promote women?

- How do the Tools of Cultural Proficiency apply to men as allies versus men as barriers?

### Personal Reaction Questions to Consider

- What is your reaction that this book is written by and about women, but *for* women and men?

- As a male educational leader, where do you see yourself on the Continuum of being an ally, mentor, and advocate?

- What might be some specific actions that you can take to strengthen the role of men in the organization as allies, mentors, and advocates?

- How have males in your organization stepped out of traditional mentoring roles to interrupt gender inequities?

## CHAPTER 7: LEADING WHILE FEMALE—A CALL FOR ACTION

### Content Questions to Consider

- As you review the rubric, where are you as an organization? Where are you as a person? What is your role in moving the organization forward on the Continuum? What is your commitment in moving yourself on the Continuum?

- Can you clearly identify the four Tools of Cultural Proficiency on the rubric and the essential role that each component holds to disrupt gender inequities in educational leadership?

- As you read the "I Am From" poem, are there ways that you might incorporate the creation of a similar poem to strengthen your circle of diversity?

### Personal Questions to Consider

- In what ways has this book informed your practices, behaviors, and roles in supporting gender equity?

- How will you use the SMART goals to assist you with action planning for the future?

- What will you do now? If not now, when will you plan your next steps?

- If not you, who?

# References

Agosto, Vonzell, & Roland, Ericka. (2018). Intersectionality and educational leadership: A critical review. *Review of Research in Education, 42*(1), 255–285.

American Association of School Administrators (AASA). (2019). Information shared at Association of California School Administrator's Annual Superintendent's Conference. Monterey, CA.

Andermahr, Sonya, Lovell, Terry, & Wolkowitz, Carol. (1997). *A concise glossary of feminist theory*. London, UK: Arnold.

Arriaga, Trudy, & Lindsey, Randall B. (2016). *Opening doors: An implementation template for cultural proficiency*. Thousand Oaks, CA: Corwin.

Bailey, Susan M. (1992). *How schools shortchange girls: The AAUW Report*. New York, NY: Marlowe & Company.

Barns, Angela. (2003). Social work, young women, and femininity. *Affilia, 18*(2), 148–164.

Blackmore, Jill. (2013). A feminist critical perspective on educational leadership. *International Journal of Leadership in Education, 16*, 139–154.

Blount, Sally. (2017, March 10). Getting more women into the c-suite means keeping them in the talent pipeline. *Kellogg Insight*. Retrieved from https://insight.kellogg.northwestern.edu/article/getting-more-women-into-the-c-suite-means-keeping-them-in-the-talent-pipeline

Bohnet, Iris. (2018). *What works: Gender equality by design*. Cambridge, MA: Belknap Press.

Brown, Brené. (2017). *Rising strong: How the ability to reset transforms the ways we live, love, parent, and lead*. New York, NY: Random House.

Brown, Jennifer. (2016). *Inclusion: Diversity, the new workplace & the will to change*. Hartford, CT: Purpose Driven.

CampbellJones, Franklin, CampbellJones, Brenda, & Lindsey, Randall B. (2010). *The cultural proficiency journey: Moving beyond ethical barriers toward profound school change*. Thousand Oaks, CA: Corwin.

Catalyst. (2018). Quick take: Women in the workforce. Retrieved from http://catalyst.org/knowledge/women-workforce-united-states

Chiefs for Change. (2019). *Report: Breaking through—Shattering the glass ceiling for women leaders*. Washington, DC.

Collins, Patricia H. (1991). *Black feminist thought: Knowledge, consciousness, and the politics of empowerment*. New York, NY: Routledge.

Collins, Patricia H. (2000). *Black feminist thought: Knowledge, consciousness, and the politics of empowerment* (2nd ed.). New York, NY: Routledge.

Collins, Patricia H. (2005). *Black sexual politics: African Americans, gender, and the new racism*. New York, NY: Routledge.

Crenshaw, Kimberlé. (1989). *Feminism in the law: Theory, practice, and criticism*. University of Chicago Legal Forum: University of Chicago.

Crenshaw, Kimberlé. (2016). *The urgency of intersectionality* [Video]. YouTube. Retrieved from https://www.youtube.com/watch? v=akOe5-UsQ2o

Cross, Terry, Bazron, Barbara, Dennis, Karl, & Isaacs, Mareasa. (1989). *Toward a culturally competent system of care* (Vol. 1). Washington, DC: Georgetown University Child Development Program, Child and Adolescent Service System Program.

Donovan, Josephine. (1993). *Feminist theory: The intellectual traditions of American feminism*. New York, NY: Continuum.

Duckett, Victoria, & Matthews, Jill. (Eds.). (2016). Archives and archivists. *Feminist Media Histories, 2*(1/Winter).

Eagly, Alice H. (2007). Female leadership advantage and disadvantage: Resolving the contradictions. *Psychology of Women Quarterly, 31*(1), 1–12.

Eagly, Alice H., Johannesen-Schmidt, Mary C., & Van Engen, Marloes L. (2003). Transformational, transactional, and laissez-faire leadership styles: A meta-analysis comparing women and men. *Psychological Bulletin, 129*(4), 569–591.

Eagly, Alice H., & Karau, Steven. (2002). Role congruity theory of prejudice toward female leaders. *Psychological Review, 109*(3), 573–598.

Eaton-Cardone, Monica. (2018). CIO Monica Eaton-Cardone examines economic benefits of women of color in tech and business [Press release]. *Marketsinsider*. Retrieved from https://markets.businessinsider.com/news/stocks/cio-monica-eaton-cardone-examines-economic-benefits-of-women-of-color-in-tech-and-business-1027474638

Evans, Judith. (1995). *Feminist theory today: An introduction to second-wave feminism*. London, UK: SAGE.

Ferguson, Ann. (1996). Can I choose who I am? And how would that empower me? Gender, race, identities, and the self. In Ann Garry & Mary Perasall (Eds.), *Women, knowledge, and reality: Exploration in feminist philosophy* (pp. 108–126). New York, NY: Routledge.

Franco, Carmella S., Ott, Maria, & Darline, P. Robles. (2011). *A culturally proficient society begins in school: Leadership for equity*. Thousand Oaks, CA: Corwin.

Fugler, J. P. (2015, July 2). Lack of women in education [Blog post]. Retrieved from https://www.huffingtonpost.com/jp-fugler/lack-of-women-in-education_b_7708220 .html

Gates, Melinda. (2019). *The moment of lift: How empowering women changes the world*. New York, NY: Flatiron Books.

Gebhardt, Jillesa. (2019). How #MeToo has impacted mentorship for women. Retrieved from https://www.surveymonkey.com/curiosity/mentor-her-2019/?% 20ut_source=mp&ut_source2=men-continue-to-pull-back-from-interacting -with-women-in-the-wake-of-metoo

Geertz, Clifford. (1973). *Thick description: Toward an interpretive theory of culture*. In *The interpretation of cultures*. New York, NY: Basic Books/HarperCollins.

Hideg, Ivona, & Shen, Winny. (2019). Why still so few? A theoretical model of the role of benevolent sexism and career support in the continued underrepresentation of women in leadership positions. *Journal of Leadership & Organizational Studies*, 26(3), 287–303.

hooks, bell. (2000). *Where we stand: Class matters*. New York: Routledge.

Hoyt, Crystal L., Johnson, Stefanie K., Murphy, Susan E., & Skinnell, Kerri H. (2010). The impact of blatant stereotype activation and group sex-composition on female leaders. *The Leadership Quarterly, 21*(5), 716–732.

Huntsberry, William. (2015, February 23). How we talk about our teachers. *NPR .org*. Retrieved from https://www.wnyc.org/story/how-we-talk-about-our-teachers/

Ibarra, Herminia, Carter, Nancy M., & Silva, Christine. (2010, September). Why men still get more promotions than women. *Harvard Business Review, 88*(5), 80–85.

Jackson, Karen, M., Chiu, Chia-Chee, Lopez, Rosita, Cleaver Simmons, Juanita M., Skria, Linda, & Warner, Linda. (2013). An exercise in tempered radicalism. In Linda C. Tillman & James J. Scheurich (Eds.), *Handbook of research on educational leadership for equity and diversity* (pp. 337–338). New York, NY: Routledge.

Jaschik, Scott. (2015, February 9). New analysis rate my professors finds patterns words used describe men and women [Blog post]. Retrieved from https://www .insidehighered.com/news/2015/02/09/new-analysis-rate-my-professors-finds -patterns-words-used-describe-men-and-women

Johnson, Brad, & Smith, David., (2018). *Athena rising: How and why men should mentor women*. New York, NY: Routledge.

Johnson, E. (1983). Reflections on black feminist therapy. In Barbara Smith (Ed.), *Home girls: A Black feminist anthology* (pp. 320–324). New York, NY: Kitchen Table—Women of Color Press.

Johnson, W. Brad, & Smith, David G. (2018, March 14). Mentoring women is not about trying to "rescue" them. *Harvard Business Review*. Retrieved from https:// hbr.org/2018/03/mentoring-women-is-not-about-trying-to-rescue-them

Kanneh, Kadiatu. (1998). Black feminisms. In Stevie Jackson & Jackie Jones (Eds.), *Contemporary feminist theories* (pp. 86–97). New York: New York University Press.

Kim, Sumi. (2008, November). Feminist discourse and the hegemonic role of mass media. *Feminist Media Studies, 8*(4), 391–406. doi:10.1080/14680770802420303

Krownapple, John. (2017). *Guiding teams to excellence with equity: Culturally proficient facilitation.* Thousand Oaks, CA: Corwin.

Kugler, Eileen Gale. (Ed.). (2012). *Innovative voices in education: Engaging diverse communities.* Summit, PA: Rowman & Littlefield Education.

Lambert, Linda, & Gardner, Mary E. (2009). *Women's ways of leading.* Indianapolis, IN: Dog Ear.

Lay, Kathy, & Daley, James. (2007). A critique of feminist theory. *Advances in Social Work, 8*(1), 49–61.

Lindsey, Delores B., Kearney, Karen M., Estrada, Delia M., Terrell, Raymond D., & Lindsey, Randall B. (2015). *Culturally proficient response to the Common Core: Ensuring equity through professional learning.* Thousand Oaks, CA: Corwin.

Lindsey, Delores B., Martinez, Richard S., Lindsey, Randall B., & Myatt, Keith T. (2020). *Culturally proficient coaching: Supporting educators to create equitable schools* (2nd ed.). Thousand Oaks, CA: Corwin.

Lindsey, Delores B., Thousand, Jacqueline S., Jew, Cynthia L., & Piowlski, Lori R. (2018). *Culturally proficient inclusive schools: All means ALL!* Thousand Oaks, CA: Corwin.

Lindsey, Randall B., Karns, Michelle S., & Myatt, Keith. (2010). *Culturally proficient education: An assets-based response to conditions of poverty.* Thousand Oaks, CA: Corwin.

Lindsey, Randall B. (2018). *The cultural proficiency manifesto: Finding clarity amidst the noise.* Thousand Oaks, CA: Corwin.

Lindsey, Randall B. (Ed.). (2012). *The best of Corwin: Equity.* Thousand Oaks, CA: Corwin.

Lindsey, Randall B., Diaz, Richard, Nuri-Robins, Kikanza, Terrell, Raymond D., & Lindsey, Delores B. (2013). *A culturally proficient response to LGBT communities: A guide for educators.* Thousand Oaks, CA: Corwin.

Lindsey, Randall B., Nuri-Robins, Kikanza, Terrell, Raymond D., & Lindsey, Delores B. (2019). *Cultural proficiency: A manual for school leaders* (4th ed.). Thousand Oaks, CA: Corwin.

Lindsey, Randall B., Roberts, Laraine M., & CampbellJones, Franklin. (2013). *The culturally proficient school: An implementation guide for school* (2nd ed.). Thousand Oaks, CA: Corwin.

MacKinnon, Catherine. (1997). Feminism, Marxism, method, and the state: An agenda for theory. In Diana Meyers (Ed.), *Feminist social thought: A reader* (pp. 65–91). New York, NY: Routledge.

MacNell, Lillian, Driscoll, Adam, & Hunt, Andrew N. (2015). What's in a name: Exposing gender bias in student ratings of teaching. *Innovative Higher Education*, 40(4), 291–303. doi:10.1007/s10755-014-9313-4

Maranto, Robert, Carroll, Kristen, Cheng, Albert, & Teodoro, Manuel P. (2018). Boys will be superintendents: School leadership as a gendered profession. *Phi Delta Kappan*, 100(2), 12–15.

Marecek, Jeanne. (2016). Invited reflection: Intersectionality theory and feminist psychology. *Psychology of Women Quarterly*, 40(2), 177–181.

Martin, Jennifer L. (2011). *Women as leaders in education: Succeeding despite inequity, discrimination, and other challenges*. Retrieved from https://ebookcentral .proquest.com

Martineau, Jennifer W., & Mount, Portia R. (2019). *Kick some glass: Ten ways women succeed at work on their own terms*. New York, NY: McGraw-Hill Education.

McGregor, Jena. (2019, May 17). #MeToo backlash: More male managers avoid mentoring women or meeting alone with them. *The Washington Post*. Retrieved from https://beta.washingtonpost.com/business/2019/05/17/metoo-backlash -more-male-managers-avoid-mentoring-women-or-meeting-alone-with-them

Menkedick, Sarah. (2019, June 9). Unsaid and unheard: The everyday importance of saying "no" to men. *Los Angeles Times*, A21.

Morey, Crystal. (2017, February 7). Women leaders in education [Blog post]. *Teaching Channel*. Retrieved from https://www.teachingchannel.org/blog/2017/02/17/ women-leaders-in-education

National Center for Education Statistics. (2018, April). Characteristics of public school teachers. Retrieved from https://nces.ed.gov/programs/coe/indicator_clr.asp

Nuri-Robins, Kikanza, & Bundy, Lewis. (2016). *Fish out of water: Mentoring, managing, and self-monitoring people who don't fit in*. Thousand Oaks, CA: Corwin.

Obama, Michelle. (2018). *Becoming*. New York, NY: Crown.

Ott, Maria. (2019). Coaching and mentoring superintendents of color. *AASA: School Administrator*, 76(8), 22–27.

Pace, Cindy. (2018, August 31). How women of color get to senior management. Retrieved from https://hbr.org/2018/08/how-women-of-color-get-to-senior -management.

Ragins, Belle Rose, & Kram, Kathy. (2007). *The handbook of mentoring at work: Theory, research, and practice*. Thousand Oaks, CA: SAGE.

Rich, Adrienne. (1986). *Blood, bread, and poetry*. New York, NY: W.W. Norton.

Robinson, Kerry, Shakeshaft, Charol, Newcomb, Whitney, & Grogan, Margaret. (2017). Necessary but not sufficient: The continuing inequality between men and women in educational leadership, findings from the AASA mid-decade survey. *Frontiers in Education, 2*(12), I–12. doi:12.3389/feduc2017.00012

Sadker, David, & Sadker, Myra. (1994). *Failing at fairness: How our schools cheat girls*. Toronto, ON: Simon & Schuster.

Sanchez-Hucles, Janis V., & Davis, Donald D. (2010). Women and women of color in leadership: Complexity, identity, and intersectionality. *American Psychologist, 65*(3), 171–181. Retrieved from https://doi-org.ezproxy.bethel.edu/10.1037/a0017459

Saulnier, Christine. (1996). *Feminist theories and social work: Approaches and application*. New York, NY: Haworth Press.

Senge, Peter, Cambron-McCabe, Helda H., Lucas, Timothy, Kleiner, Art, Dutton, Janis, & Smith, Bryan. (2000). *Schools that learn: A fifth discipline fieldbook for educators, parents, and everyone who cares about education*. New York, NY: Doubleday.

Smith, Hannah. (2013). Raising Shakespeare's sister: Or why we need to talk about female speakers in search [Blog post.] Retrieved from https://www.stateofdigital.com/female-speakers-in-search/

Stempel, Christiane R., Rigotti, Thomas, & Mohr, Gisela. (2015). Think transformational leadership—Think female? *Leadership, 11*(3), 259–280.

Stephens, Diana L., & Lindsey, Randall B. (2011). *Culturally proficient collaboration: Use and misuse of school counselors*. Thousand Oaks, CA: Corwin.

Sud, Shruti, & Amanesh, Apurv. (2019, January 4). Breaking glass ceiling in leadership roles. Retrieved from https://www.shrm.org/shrm-india/pages/breaking-glass-ceiling-in-leadership-roles.aspx

Superville, Denisa. (2016). Few women run the nation's school districts. Why? Retrieved from www.edweek.org/ew/artivles/2016/few-women-run-the-nations-school-districts.html

Tan, Kevin, Oe, Jin Shin, & Le, Minh Dung Hoang. (2018). How does gender relate to social skills? Exploring differences in social skills mindsets, academics, and behaviors among high-school freshmen students. *Psychology in the Schools, 55*(4), 429–442.

Taylor, Edward, Gillborn, David, & Ladson-Billings, Gloria. (Eds.). (2009). *Foundations of critical race theory in education*. New York, NY: Routledge.

Theoharis, George. (2007). Social justice educational leaders and resistance: Toward a theory of social justice leadership. *Educational Administration Quarterly, 43*(2), 221–258.

Travis, Dnika J., Thorpe-Moscon, Jennifer, & McCluney, Courtney. (2018, February 15). Day-to-day experiences of emotional tax among women and men of color in the workplace. *Catalyst*. Retrieved from https://www.catalyst.org/research/day-to-day-experiences-of-emotional-tax-among-women-and-men-of-color-in-the-workplace/

Tulshyan, Ruchika. (2015, February 10). Speaking up as a woman of color at work [Blog post]. Retrieved from https://www.forbes.com/sites/ruchikatulshyan/2015/02/10/speaking-up-as-a-woman-of-color-at-work/#3d06bba32ea3

Wallace, Teresa. (2014). Increasing the proportion of female superintendents in the 21st century. *Advancing Women in Leadership*, *34*, 48–53.

Williams, Christine. (1992). The glass escalator: Hidden advantages for men in the "female" professions. *Social Problems, 39*(3), 253–257.

Williams, Christine. (2013). The glass escalator, revisited: Gender inequality in neo-liberal times. *Gender & Society, 27*(5), 609–629. doi:10.1177/0891243213490232

Wyland, Catherine. (2016). Underrepresentation of females in the superintendency in Minnesota. *Planning and Changing*, *47*(1), 47–62.

Yanow, Wendy. (2011). Book review: Taylor, Edward, Gillborn, David., & Ladson-Billings, Gloria. (Eds.). (2009). *Foundations of critical race theory in education.* New York, NY: Routledge. *Adult Education Quarterly, 61*(2), 198–199.

Zalis, Shelley. (2019, March 6). Power of the pack: Women who support women are more successful. *Forbes*. Retrieved from https://www.forbes.com/sites/shelleyzalis/2019/03/06/power-of-the-pack-women-who-support-women-are-more-successful/#326c61d61771

# Index

Hideg, Ivona, 76–77
Homelife, struggles with, 95–96
Hooks, bell, 79
Hoskins, Juanita, 26
Hostile sexism, 13, 81
Hunt, Andrew N., 40

Ibarra, Herminia, 6, 7
Inside-out awareness, 18, 43
Institutionalizing Cultural Knowledge, 50, 108 (table)
Interruptors, men as, 90–92
Intersectionality, 27, 66, 80–81, 83–85

*Kick Some Glass: 10 Ways Women Succeed at Work on Their Own Terms*, 7
King, Martin Luther, Jr., 25
Kram, Kathy, 93

Labyrinth, 85
Lambert, Linda, 59, 99, 100
Lamott, Anne, 18
Le, Minh Dung Hoang, 55
LeaningIn, 4
LGBTQIA+ persons, 14, 59, 61
Lifelong learning, 31–32, 101
Lindsey, Delores B., 45
Lyons, George Ella, 113

MacNell, Lillian, 40
Macroaggressions, 85–88
Managing the Dynamics of Difference, 50, 107 (table)
Martineau, Jennifer W., 7
Men
   importance of support for women by, 8–10
   as interrupters, allies, advocates, and mentors, stories of, 90–92
   leadership differences between women and, 66–68
   as mentors for women, 4, 6, 64–65, 93
   privileges of white, 36–37
   recommending actions for all, 93–97
Mentoring, 4, 6, 90–92, 93, 101
   defined, 12
   important allies in, 64–65
   of women by women, 102
#MeToo movement, 4, 37, 70

Microaggressions, 85–88
Mid-career marathon, 95–96
Morey, Crystal, 44
Morrison, Toni, 1
Mount, Portia R., 7

Narrative data, 58–59
Networking, 74, 96–97
Nonbinary persons, 13
Nuri-Robins, Kikanza, 26

Obama, Barack, 90
Obama, Michelle, 19, 100, 109
Odegard, Florence, 26
Oe, Jin Shin, 55
Oppression and entitlement, systems of, 60–61
Ott, Maria, 41

Pace, Cindy, 86
Pathways, 13
Pipelines, 13
Pitfalls, 13, 108

Ragins, Belle Rose, 93
Rate My Professor, 41
Resistance to change, 63–64

Sadker, David, 56
Sadker, Myra, 56
Sandberg, Sheryl, 4
Schmidt, Benjamin M., 41
Senge, Peter, 38
Sexism, 13, 36, 81
   educational, 56
   systemic, 40–41
Shen, Winny, 76–77
Sponsors, 13
Stories
   barriers and, 58–59
   changing the system by telling new, 21
   as counternarratives, 21–33
   current, 20–21
   Delores's, 28–33
   faux, 18–19
   of men as interrupters, allies, advocates, and mentors, 90–92
   power of, 18–19
   Stacy's, 25–28
   Trudy's, 21–25

A SAGE Publishing Company

**CORWIN HAS ONE MISSION:** to enhance education through intentional professional learning.

We build long-term relationships with our authors, educators, clients, and associations who partner with us to develop and continuously improve the best evidence-based practices that establish and support lifelong learning.

## THE PROFESSIONAL LEARNING ASSOCIATION

Learning Forward is a nonprofit, international membership association of learning educators committed to one vision in K–12 education: Excellent teaching and learning every day. To realize that vision, Learning Forward pursues its mission to build the capacity of leaders to establish and sustain highly effective professional learning. Information about membership, services, and products is available from www.learningforward.org.

# Solutions YOU WANT | Experts YOU TRUST | Results YOU NEED

EVENTS

>>> **INSTITUTES**

Corwin Institutes provide large regional events where educators collaborate with peers and learn from industry experts. Prepare to be recharged and motivated!

**corwin.com/institutes**

ON-SITE PD

>>> **ON-SITE PROFESSIONAL LEARNING**

Corwin on-site PD is delivered through high-energy keynotes, practical workshops, and custom coaching services designed to support knowledge development and implementation.

**corwin.com/pd**

>>> **PROFESSIONAL DEVELOPMENT RESOURCE CENTER**

The PD Resource Center provides school and district PD facilitators with the tools and resources needed to deliver effective PD.

**corwin.com/pdrc**

ONLINE

>>> **ADVANCE**

Designed for K–12 teachers, Advance offers a range of online learning options that can qualify for graduate-level credit and apply toward license renewal.

**corwin.com/advance**

**Contact a PD Advisor at (800) 831-6640 or visit www.corwin.com for more information**